Pebble Pets

30 lovable companions crafted from pebbles and paper

Steve & Megumi Biddle

D&C
David and Charles
www.mycraftivity.com

A DAVID & CHARLES BOOK
Copyright © David & Charles Limited 2009

David & Charles is an F+W Media Inc. company
4700 East Galbraith Road
Cincinnati, OH 45236

First published in the UK in 2009

Text, designs and illustrations copyright
© Steve & Megumi Biddle 2009
Photography copyright © David and Charles 2009

Steve & Megumi Biddle have asserted their
right to be identified as authors of this work
in accordance with the Copyright, Designs
and Patents Act, 1988.

A catalogue record for this book is available
from the British Library.

ISBN-13: 978-0-7153-3175-0 paperback
ISBN-10: 0-7153-3175-2 paperback

Printed in China by RR Donnelley
for David & Charles
Brunel House   Newton Abbot   Devon

Senior Commissioning Editor: Cheryl Brown
Editors: Bethany Dymond and Emily Rae
Art Editor: Sarah Clark
Production Controller: Kelly Smith
Photographers: Karl Adamson and Kim Sayer

Visit our website at www.davidandcharles.co.uk

David & Charles books are available from all
good bookshops; alternatively you can contact
our Orderline on 0870 9908222 or write to us
at FREEPOST EX2 110, D&C Direct, Newton
Abbot, TQ12 4ZZ (no stamp required UK only);
US customers call 800-289-0963 and Canadian
customers call 800-840-5220.

Contents

Introduction

Discover the exciting world of *Pebble Pets*; use simple papercraft techniques to recreate the character of your favourite pet with a realistic pebble keepsake that will sit in the palm of your hand and make a great desktop companion.

You will be spoilt for choice with this irresistible range of over 30 animal designs, from Perfect Pets including guinea pigs, rabbits and rats, to an adorable range of Desirable Dogs and Coveted Cats. Popular canine breeds range from the strong and muscular Shiba Inu to the sleek black and tan dachshund, whilst feline friends include a tortoiseshell moggy, and the Siamese and Japanese bobtail breeds, each posed in a delightful range of realistic poses. Each section also presents all of the essential accessories that your pets will need, including fabulous food bowls, cushions, toys and collars.

Each project provides easy-to-follow step-by-step instructions on how to create a range of lovable creatures. The body and head of each pet are made from small pebbles, carefully chosen and covered with paper using a simple layering technique. Ears are created from stiffened paper or card, and facial details are constructed using modelling clay. You can have fun creating your pets in a variety of different poses, whether they are causing mischief at play, curled up in a ball asleep, or simply sitting up watching the world go by.

Perfect Pets: discover how to work from a single pebble to build up your pet's fur colouring, ears, nose and tail.

Desirable Dogs: learn how to join two pebbles together and add the nose, ears and tail to create the perfect pooch.

Using this Book

The opening section (pages 6–23) introduces you to the most essential object that can be easily found, a pebble, and lists the basic tools and materials that you will need to get started. Discover the simple techniques of covering your pebble with pieces of handmade paper, giving your pets a firm foundation, joining head and body pebbles, and moulding your pebble pet's facial details, ears and tails in a realistic way.

As you work through the projects section, you will find an assortment of delightful animals, starting with Perfect Pets (pages 24–57) and progressing to Desirable Dogs (pages 58–101), before you enter the charming world of Coveted Cats (pages 102–125). Each project lists all the materials you will need, with irresistible photographs and clear step-by-step illustrations to help you to achieve the perfect pebble pet. You'll also find a variety of ideas to enable you to adapt and personalize the projects and extend the range of pebble possibilities, including a stunning range of quick-to-make accessory projects.

We do hope that *Pebble Pets* will introduce you to a craft of absorbing interest and that you will develop many creative skills and the confidence to experiment. The pets in this book have given us many pleasurable hours and we are certain that they will do the same for you.

Steve and Megumi

Designer Profile

During her childhood and while living on the family farm, in Hokkaido, North Japan, Megumi Biddle learned a range of traditional Japanese paper arts from her grandmother, especially how to make dolls and other figures by covering carved wooden shapes, pebbles and shells with pieces of handmade paper.

As a lover of animals and nature, Megumi was motivated, later on in her life, to interpret a creature's behaviour by means of developing an original style of pebble-covering artistry and so creating the enchanting projects that can be found within Pebble Pets.

Coveted Cats: use two pebbles to recreate a number of realistic poses and add facial details to your feline friends.

Accessories: treat your pet with some creature comforts, whether it is a fabulous collar, a cosy cushion or a fun toy.

Pebble Basics

The most important aspect of creating the perfect pebble pet is to find the ideal pebble. Pebbles are so easy to obtain and by following our simple guidelines below, it is simple to find or create the right pebble shape to achieve a realistic look.

Spoilt for Choice

Pebbles Everywhere

Mother Nature has created a huge variety of pebbles, each unique in their size and texture. Many different types of pebbles are just lying around, waiting to be discovered and turned into an adorable pet keepsake. You may find that the ideal location for finding the perfect sized pebble is your very own back garden!

If you live in a built-up area, try your local garden centre or home improvement store, where you might be able to pick your own pebbles. Craft and hobby stores also often supply already washed pebbles of many shapes and sizes by the bag. Keep your eyes open at all times, you never know where an interestingly shaped pebble will appear, however do not take any pebbles from a neighbour's garden (without asking permission first), or from any beach, national park or conservation area.

In the early stages of making pebble pets, it is better to start with a larger sized pebble than the one suggested in the pet's pebble focus. Once you have built up your confidence you may move on to smaller and more interestingly shaped pebbles. Hold the pebble in your hand; slowly turn it around and look for the best angle for the most suitable pose. You never know, you might come up with a new and unexpected result and develop an entirely original pebble pet.

Size Matters

If you are unable to find pebbles of the required dimensions, look for pebbles nearest to our suggestions and use the techniques on page 8 (A Firm Foundation) to give them the necessary proportions.

For your pet's body, your pebble should sit steadily and securely and be round and smooth in appearance without any breaks, cracks or missing chunks. The pebble for the pet's head should be similar to a slightly flattened ball and should be about a third of the size of the pebble used for the body so that they are in proportion with each other. For a puppy or kitten, the head pebble should be approximately half the size of the pebble used for the body. Try to use oval shaped pebbles for dogs and rounded pebbles for cats.

Before you begin to work on your pebble and to prevent any dirty smudges appearing on the finished pet, remove any soil and grease from the pebble's surface by submerging it overnight in a mixture of warm water and washing-up liquid. Any stubborn matter can be removed by scrubbing its surface with an old toothbrush. Pat it dry by using a tea towel or paper towels.

The projects in *Pebble Pets* each require a pebble about the size of a hen's egg that will sit comfortably in the palm of your hand. See the pebble focus feature at the beginning of each project for any specific requirements for each individual pet. This is a guideline to follow only and if you find it difficult to find the perfect size pebble for your chosen pet, try to find the nearest one to fit your requirements.

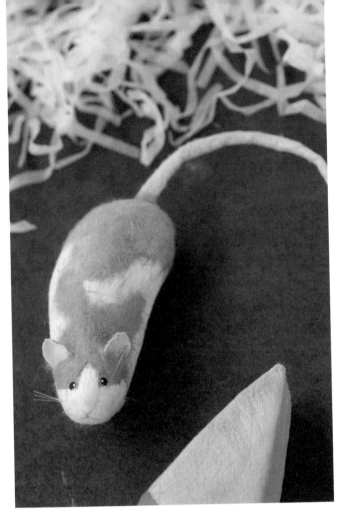

To give this rat (pages 38–43) an interesting pose, you will need one stretched bean-shaped pebble that is slightly curved to one side.

For the Westie's body (pages 80–83), you will need a teardrop-shaped pebble with a slightly flat base, so it will sit up without wobbling. To get the head in proportion, use one round pebble, approximately half the size of the body pebble.

For the Siamese's sleek body (pages 110–113), you will need one tall triangular teardrop-shaped pebble that is slightly twisted to one side. For the head, use one flattish circular-shaped pebble, approximately one-third of the size of the pebble used for the body.

A Firm Foundation

No matter how hard you look, you may find it difficult to obtain the perfect pebble to fit your requirements. An ideal solution is to grab the nearest pebble and fill up any indents or cracks with pieces of modelling clay to create a smooth surface to work from. If at first you don't succeed, simply remove the clay with a damp cloth and start all over again.

1 The pebble that we have chosen is rectangular in shape, and would make an ideal body for a dog. However, it is a little scratched, has a few indents and is a little wobbly at the base where we would like it to sit or stand.

2 The solution is to fill up any imperfections by using small pieces of modelling clay to smooth the surface and ensure that the pebble's base is reasonably level. Smooth the clay so that it is flat and once it is dry you should have an even, secure surface to work from.

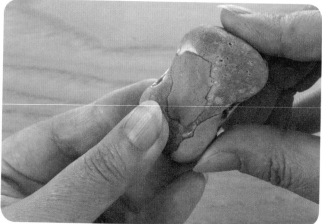

3 Add an egg-like shaped pebble for a head and you will be on your way to creating the perfect Schnauzer or Scottie dog.

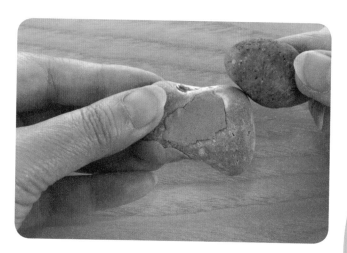

The schnauzer (pages 76–79) sits solidly on his long, thin rectangular shaped pebble which creates a firm base to work from.

Perfect Poses

Learning how a pebble's shape can be transformed into a desired pet is a technique that will develop with practice and time. Follow the useful information below to help you choose the correctly shaped pebble for your project.

Sitting Straight

A kidney bean-shaped pebble with one end smaller than the other will help to create a pet's spinal line. This can be used for most of the single pebble Perfect Pets, including the rabbits, pigs and guinea pigs.

Begging for Food

Pebbles that stand up in an almost triangular-like appearance are ideal for creating the body of a sitting up pet, such as a kitten or puppy. The pebble used for the pet's head should resemble a slightly flattened ball in shape and should be approximately half the size of the pebble used for the body.

Dozing Pose

A broad bean-shaped pebble that slightly curves upwards is ideal for creating the body of dozing pets such as cats or dogs. The pebble used for the pet's head should be similar in shape to a slightly flattened ball and is ideally about a third of the size of the pebble used for the body.

Curled Up Asleep

A pebble with a slightly downwards curve is perfect for creating a sleeping pet, such as a cat or dog. The pebble used for the pet's head should be egg-like in shape and approximately a third of the size of the pebble used for the body.

Papers

There are many different types of handmade and craft papers available, varying from patterned or plain and textured or smooth. These can be found locally in specialist Asian gift shops, stationery stores or at art and craft suppliers, or you can use a mail-order service or the Internet (see Suppliers, page 126). You will find that most papers come pre-packaged in A5 (21 x 15cm/8¼ x 5¾in) rectangles. This size is perfect for the pebble pets, as you only need small amounts of paper for their construction. All the pebble pets in this book are made using solid coloured handmade papers that are as near to the exact fur colouring of the pet as possible. However, if it's impossible for you to obtain the correct coloured handmade paper, why not let your imagination run wild and create a flower patterned pig or pink-dotted Dalmatian?

Handmade paper
is a softer, more fabric-like material than machine-made paper. Medium strength Japanese washi paper, known as 'Kozo', and other handmade papers from around the world are left in a natural hue, given a solid colour or tie-dyed to create a pattern which repeats itself when the paper is unfolded.

Pink facial tissues
are single tissues that are used for each pebble pet's facial detail and occasionally for their tails.

Craft paper
is available in many colours, types and weights. Use white craft paper to reinforce the pets' ears. Pets' eyes are punched out of black craft paper, or dark pink craft paper if the pet has white fur. For making a pet's collar you could even use reptile skin gift-wrap.

Dyeing Handmade Paper

Nowadays a large variety of coloured handmade papers are widely available, but occasionally you may find it difficult to find a particular colour to match your requirements. An easy solution is to buy rectangles of white handmade paper and dye them to the required colour using fabric dyes or coloured inks that are obtainable from art and craft suppliers, using the following instructions:

1 Mix the fabric dye or coloured ink with a little water in a dish or bowl to control the overall strength of the tint colour. (Note: the tint is slightly lighter when dry.)

2 Crinkle up the white handmade paper and submerge it into the mixture. Let the paper sit for a few seconds – any longer and it could turn into a lump of papier mâché. Wearing rubber kitchen gloves, remove the paper and tightly squeeze out any excess liquid.

3 Gently unfold the paper and lay it out on top of a few sheets of newspaper to dry.

Crimping Handmade Paper

Even though a piece of handmade paper is very flexible when glue is applied to its surface, it can still be difficult to glue it around a three-dimensional object like a pebble. You may be lucky enough to find a specialized type of Japanese handmade paper called *'Kyosei-shi'* or *'Momi-gami'*, which has been 'crimped' at its source of manufacture, making it extremely pliable. As most Western art and craft shops supply handmade paper in uncrimped flat sheets, you will find the following technique an easy way to crimp a rectangle of paper to create a malleable surface to work from.

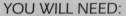

YOU WILL NEED:
- One 1 or 1.5cm diameter x 20cm (⅜ or ⅝in diameter x 8in) length of dowel or any similar sized round object with a smooth surface
- A rectangle of handmade paper to be crimped

1 Place the rectangle of handmade paper lengthways on. Turn the length of dowel horizontally and place it on top of the paper's bottom edge. Loosely roll the paper up around the dowel from bottom to top.

2 Stand the dowel and rolled up paper vertically, placing one end onto a flat surface. To prevent the paper from unrolling, hold its free end between the thumb and forefinger of one hand and with the other hand, push or slide the paper all the way down the dowel, crimping it in the process.

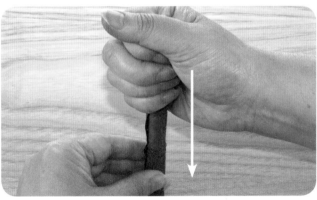

3 Gently unroll the paper. Repeat steps 1 and 2 a few more times, to crimp the paper evenly all over.

4 Repeat steps 1 to 3 with the rectangle of paper placed sideways on to crimp the paper in the opposite direction. When the paper is finally opened out, it will be stretchable and the texture of its surface will be like velvet to the touch.

Basic Tool Kit

There is nothing particularly specialized about the equipment for making the projects in this book. You will probably already have some of the items you need, and no doubt if you do have to buy anything new you will be able to re-use it for other crafting projects. There is no need to stick rigidly to the tools that we have recommended and if you have a particular tool that you are happy with, then by all means use it. The important thing is that it works for you.

Tools of the Trade

It is a good plan to begin by assembling a basic tool kit because this is the equipment you will use again and again. We have built up our tool kit over several years and we are constantly adding to it. The items listed here are found in our tool kit and were used to create the projects in this book. You will need additional items for each project as well as the appropriate paper or card, and these are listed with the project instructions.

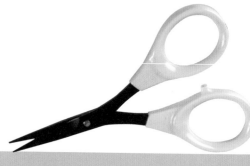

• **Pencils** for marking out the spinal line and position of the ears, eyes and mouth of your pebble pets. Use a 2B pencil so that you can easily erase any mistakes.

• **Brush-tip pens** are useful for adding detail and marking on facial features. Use a grey pen for adding on a light furred pet's eyes, mouth and other facial details and a black one for darker furred pets.

• **Paw-print pens** have a nib in the shape of a paw. Ideal for decorating any surface when simply dotted around.

• **Felt-tip pens** in black and brown are ideal for adding on fine details.

• **Very fine paintbrush** for applying details with paint. Clean immediately after use with the appropriate solvent.

• **Modelling spatula** for handling any pieces of modelling clay. The spatula's rounded end is useful for creating a pet's cup-like ears (see page 20).

• **Vellum embossing tool** of a medium size is recommended for pressing into the edges of a cat's chin, lips and nose to define its image and for indenting the whiskers gluing position.

• **Ruler** for measuring and marking out. A steel ruler or one with a metal edge is useful for tearing paper against.

• **Needlework scissors** are useful for intricate work and for marking out tiny pieces of paper.

• **Compasses** are great for marking out perfect circles. Use an old set when marking out circles of modelling clay.

• **Tweezers** can be useful for pressing a pet's small facial features, such as eyes, nose and whiskers, into place and for picking up and positioning small punched paper shapes. Keep the grabbing surfaces free from glue.

• **Short length of dowel** is useful for crimping handmade paper (see page 11). Any other rounded object, such as an unsharpened pencil, plastic tube or metal rod, can be used as long as it has a smooth surface.

• **Tube of white acrylic paint** for adding tiny dots of paint onto a pet's eyes to create the impression of a reflection of light.

Exciting Embellishments

Enhancing your projects with embellishments is the best part of creating pebble pets. Scan the aisles of your local craft shop and experiment with the vast array of colourful items that they have to offer. Store your accessories in self-seal plastic bags to keep them clean and organized. Here are some of the items that we have found useful:

- **Decorative paper punches** are ideal for creating a pet's eyes from a piece of black craft paper. Try to find a punch in the shape of a teardrop or a small circle. Hold the punch upside down, so that you can more easily see where you are placing it.

- **Florists' wires** come in a large range of thicknesses (gauges). Use a white covered 24-gauge wire; perfect for strengthening a pet's tail and in the creation of accessories such as the fishbone and some toys.

- **Sticky-backed gems** come in an endless variety of colours, shapes and textures, and they are ideal for adding a little sparkle to a pet's collar.

- **Small bells** are readily available and can be added to collars to give frivolous charm to any pebble pet.

- **Small, coloured, brass paper fasteners** make the perfect identity disc for your pet's collar, when fastened into place by opening out its prongs.

- **Clear nail varnish** for painting over a pet's eyes and nose to make them shiny, bold and life-like.

- **Glue mix (wallpaper paste)** comes in a powder form and is obtainable from DIY stores. It is the ideal adhesive for attaching handmade paper onto your pebbles, as it enables the paper to stretch. Mix a small amount together with a little water to make a paste, the consistency of which should be lumpy and stay on your fingertip. Add an equal quantity of PVA to make a mixture that becomes almost clear and not shiny when dry.

- **PVA adhesive** is a safe, ready-mixed white solution adhesive that becomes invisible when dry. It creates a strong bond when dry and therefore is the perfect adhesive to use when attaching a pet's various body parts together.

- **Glue stick** is a clean, quick and safe glue that is ideal for most light paperwork e.g. when gluing small fur patches and spots onto a pebble pet.

- **Gluing surface** for protecting your worktop when you are using glue or adhesive. Place a large sheet of cardboard under your project and take great care to glue in small sections.

- **Dish and cling film** for making and containing your glue mix.

- **Two cotton hand towels** for use when gluing. Keep one towel wet and the other dry, so that you can wipe any sticky fingers clean on the wet towel and then quickly dry them before moving on.

- **Beading thread or clear nylon fishing line** is used for creating a pet's whiskers. Cut three strands of either material to the same length as the width of the pet's body.

- **White cotton wool** is the perfect material for making and adding thickness to a pet's tail and creating various pet accessories.

- **Air-dry modelling clay** is available in brown, grey or white. It is easy to roll and mould. Use it for correcting a pebble's shape, creating a pet's nose and in making most of the accessories. Roll out any clay on top of a few sheets of slightly damped kitchen towels to prevent it from sticking to your work surface.

Basic Techniques

A sound knowledge of the following basic papercrafting techniques lies behind the success of any creative achievement, so it is well worth getting to grips with these methods before making a start on your projects. Learn to observe the areas of fur, patches and bands of colour in the ears, face and body of the animal that you want to portray to allow you to get your pebble proportions as accurate as possible.

This section explains the fundamental techniques required to make the pebble pets that follow. Some of the techniques are explained in step-by-step detail, while others are simply previewed here, referring you on to step-by-step guidelines provided in the project chapters. For example, you will find instructions on the covering of a foundation pebble with top paper to create the fur in Guinea Pigs chapter (pages 26–31).

Cover Up

The basic technique to making up any pebble pet is to start by completely covering your pebble with torn pieces of crimped white handmade paper or the appropriately fur coloured crimped handmade paper before progressing onto building up layers of fur if required. Before covering your pebble, you can also add a small knob of clay to its pointed end to create the pet's nose.

As the colours of the papers required for the fur varies from pet to pet, details of these will be given in the you will need section and relevant project instructions for each pet. Instructions on how to crimp a piece of handmade paper can be found on page 11. Generally, the attachment of the paper to a pebble is as follows:

1 **To create a glue mix**, make up a small amount of wallpaper paste that is lumpy in consistency. Add an equal quantity of PVA adhesive and mix it into a smooth paste to make an ideal mix for attaching handmade paper onto your pebble. While not in use, cover the dish with a piece of cling film to prevent the mix from drying hard.

2 Tear out a rectangle from crimped handmade paper, with its width being slightly shorter than the pebble's length and its length the same size as the pebble's circumference.

3 Using the tip of your forefinger, apply the glue mix made in step 1 to the handmade paper, working it evenly from the centre of the paper out towards and over the torn edges.

4 Gently pick up the handmade paper from your work surface. Turn it sideways on with its glued side face down. Holding the pebble lengthways on, carefully wrap the paper around it, while at the same time stretching the paper so that it fits the pebble's contours, as shown. Gently press the paper's overlap and its edges neatly down.

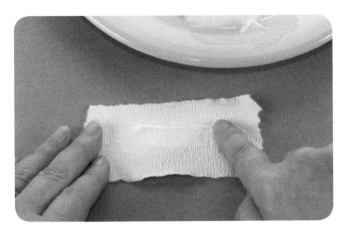

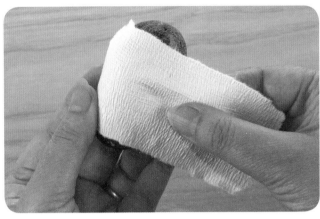

5 Tear out two round pieces from the rectangle of crimped handmade paper. One piece must be large enough to cover the pebble's 'front-end' and the other its 'back-end'. Repeat step 3 with each piece.

6 Attach the round pieces of handmade paper to their respective ends of the pebble.

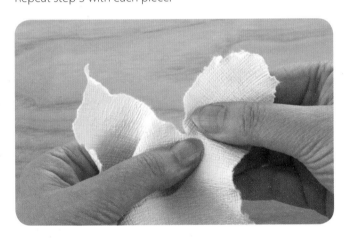

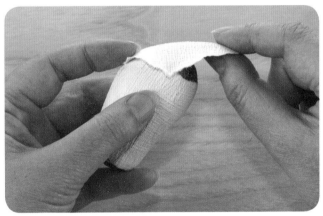

7 Roll the pebble between the palms of your hands to neatly smooth down the handmade paper and remove any air bubbles in the process.

8 Place the covered pebble to one side to dry. Once dry, use a pencil to lightly mark the line of the pet's spine, working from the pebble's back-end to its front-end, as shown.

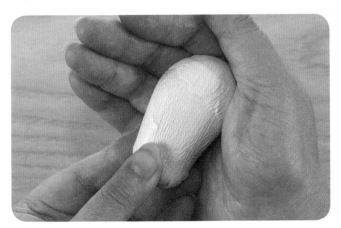

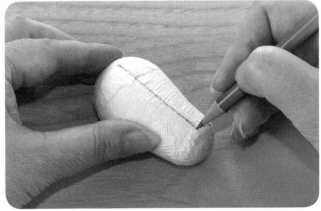

Fun with Fur

Handmade papers are the most beautiful of all papers. They come in a fabulous range of colours, however it is their different textures and surfaces that set them apart from machine-made papers and make them the perfect material to use when creating the fur of a pebble pet.

Remember when applying a pebble pet's fur that it radiates away from the nose, continuing all the way to the tip of the tail. When tearing handmade paper, tear it little by little between your thumbs and forefingers and avoid ripping it in one continuous action. This will also enable the paper's fibres to protrude like strands of hair, hence suggesting a pet's fur. If you are not happy with your first attempt at making a pebble pet's fur, simply give the pet a bath by soaking it in warm water. Most of the paper will come off easily and any remaining material can be quickly scraped away. Dry your pebble and start all over again.

Aim to copy the pets exactly as they appear in the photographs, but remember that the work of no two artists is alike. What is important is your own unique, personal touch, as these are the feelings and life that you inject into your projects. These tangible qualities will allow the pebble pets to 'speak for themselves'. Be inspired to have a go at creating a range of realistic fur coats for your pebble pets, some of which are previewed here.

Graduating Colours

A large variety of animals display a graduation fur colouring, such as the golden hamster. To create such an effect, tear rectangles of the appropriately coloured handmade papers into pieces the same size as the areas to be covered. Attach them into place using the glue mix, while at the same time making sure that they slightly overlap one another. Where the pieces overlap, use the tips of your fingers to lightly feather the paper's fibres rather than leaving stark edges.

Patched Patterns

Many pets have areas of patched fur, such as the guinea pig. To create such an effect, tear small pieces of the appropriately coloured handmade papers. Using the glue mix, attach them randomly onto the pet's body.

Brilliant Bands

The Dutch rabbit is coloured similarly at the front and back, with a broad band of white around the front part of its body up to the head. To create this banded effect, tear pieces of the appropriately coloured handmade papers into the required sizes. Attach them over the pet's front and back portions using the glue mix, leaving the relevant area white to create a band of fur.

Simply Spotty

To create an animal's spots, use a paper punch or pair of scissors to produce a quantity of small circles out of the appropriately coloured handmade paper. Attach them onto the body randomly using a glue stick. When gluing on a Dalmatian's spots, avoid symmetry by placing some of them in random clusters of twos and threes for a natural look.

Two-Toned

The fur of many varieties of animals, such as the black and tan dachshund, is two-toned. To create this striking effect, tear pieces of the appropriately coloured handmade paper into the required sizes. Attach them into place using the glue mix, to cover the pebble's top area with one colour and its base with another.

Striped Wonder

Many creatures display stripes of different coloured fur running along their back. The chipmunk has black stripes with brown edges and white in-between. To create such an effect, tear the appropriately coloured handmade papers into strips of the required length. Using a glue stick, attach them onto the animal's body.

Joining Pebbles

The cat and dog pebble pets included are made up from two pebbles, using a larger pebble for the body and a smaller pebble for the head. It is easy to join two pebbles together by adding a paper ring once they have been covered with handmade paper. Guidance for the positioning of the paper ring is given in the pebble focus feature at the start of each project.

1 Use a pencil, ruler and scissors to mark, measure and cut out a 1 x 6cm (⅜ x 2⅜in) rectangle of the appropriately coloured handmade paper. Smear glue mix all over the paper. Turn the paper sideways on with its glued side on top and tightly twist it up diagonally from bottom right to top left between your thumbs and forefingers to make a length of paper string.

2 Bend the paper string into a ring-like shape while overlapping its ends slightly. Pinch them securely together. Apply PVA adhesive onto the neck area, in the place you wish to attach the head. Carefully place the ring on top.

3 Apply PVA adhesive to the ring and gently sit the head on top. When you are satisfied with the head's position, hold both pebbles firmly together until the adhesive is dry. As the head pebble can be a little heavy it might have the tendency to fall off every now and again – be patient and wait until both pebbles are strongly fastened to the ring and each other, before letting go.

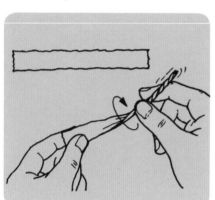

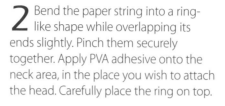

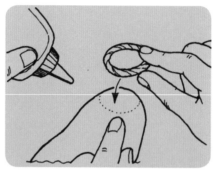

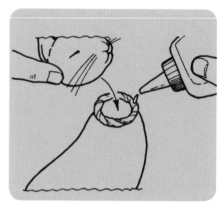

Colourful Collars

To hide the join between the head and body pebbles, a collar or ribbon is fastened around the pets' necks. This can be created in any colour you like and it is easy to add embellishments, such as diamanté gems, nametags, fasteners, or even a cute little bell, making this a fashionable as well as functional addition to your pet.

Your pebble pet will wear their name with pride with this simple nametag (see page 97).

Twist handmade paper and tie it around the pet's neck in a reef (square) knot for an elegant look (see page 123).

Add a little sparkle to this collar by decorating the surface of the collar with tiny sticky-backed gems (see page 97).

For the smartest of pets, dress to impress with this classic bowtie (see page 98).

Typical Tails

Tails come in all shapes and sizes, however a pebble pet's tail is generally created from a length of 24-gauge white covered florists' wire, which is padded with cotton wool and covered by a piece of the appropriately coloured handmade paper. Use a small piece of handmade paper to hide the join between the tail and body while at the same time securing it in place. As the tail construction and its attachment can vary from pet to pet, further explanations will be given in the relevant project instructions.

Curly Wurly

A curly, kinked or straight tail for a pig, mouse or rat is simply made up from a length of florists' wire, which is then covered with the appropriately coloured handmade paper. As the wire's length can vary from pet to pet exact measurements will be given in the relevant project instructions.

Long and Curved

For a cat or chipmunk, you will need to create a curved tail that follows the shape of its body. The tail is made from a length of florists' wire, which is wrapped with cotton wool to pad it out slightly, then covered with the appropriately coloured handmade paper.

Happy and Wagging

Dogs' tails are curved from just beyond the bottom of their haunches and angled up slightly. Most of the dogs' tails are made from a length of florists' wire, which is then covered with the appropriately coloured handmade paper.

Short and Fluffy

The rabbit's fluffy pom-pom tail is made from a small ball of cotton wool, which is then wrapped in the appropriately coloured handmade paper. Use a little PVA adhesive when attaching the tail to the underside of the rabbit's back-end.

Ear We Go!

Pebble pets' ears come in all shapes and sizes, from the little stubby ears of a hamster to the long, slender ears of a rabbit. Use your imagination when creating a pet's ears, but you should be aware that the dimensions of the ear pieces will depend upon the proportions of the pebbles that you have chosen for your pet. You should aim to keep the ears in balance with the pet's head and body.

As the ear shape and its attachment to the head can vary from pet to pet, further explanations will be given in the relevant project instructions and templates for a pet's ears are always provided. However, generally the construction of a pet's ears is similar to the guidelines for making the ginger cat's ears that follow.

Making Up the Ginger Cat's Ears

YOU WILL NEED:
- two 3 x 4cm (1⅛ x 1½in) rectangles of handmade paper: one in ginger for the outer ear and one in pink for the inner ear
- one 3 x 4cm (1⅛ x 1½in) rectangle of white craft paper
- glue mix
- PVA adhesive
- basic tool kit (see pages 12–13)

1 Attach the white craft paper onto the pink handmade paper using the glue mix. Draw two acorn-like shapes approximately one-half of the cat's forehead in size (templates are provided on page 106). Cut them out.

2 Tear out two slightly larger acorn-like shapes from the ginger handmade paper. Using the glue mix, attach them onto the white side of the ears made in step 1 to sandwich the craft paper between the two pieces of handmade paper.

3 When the glue is dry, place an ear on the palm of your hand with the inner ear side on top. Using a round-headed spatula, press down and around from the tip of the ear towards its centre, making the ear cup-like in appearance. Repeat with the remaining ear.

4 Place the ears with their inner ear side facing upwards. Pour a little PVA adhesive into each of their lower sections. Attach them onto each side the cat's head at the back and use small pieces of ginger handmade paper to hide the join between the ears and head, while at the same time securing them in place. Once the adhesive is dry, lift the ears up slightly by carefully bending them at their base, and mould them into a curved triangular-like shape.

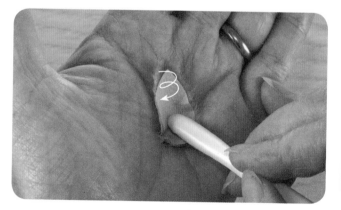

Small, Narrow Ears

A few pets' ears, such as those of the chipmunk, mouse, rabbit and rat, are very small or narrow, making it almost impossible for you to tear the handmade paper as in step 2 on page 20. The solution is to layer and glue the three rectangles of paper together as in step 1, while making sure to sandwich the white craft paper between the handmade papers. Use a pair of scissors to cut the handmade paper into the required shapes as indicated in the appropriate template and repeat step 3. As the ear attachment to the head can vary from pet to pet, further explanations will be given in the relevant project instructions.

Whose Ears Are These?

Pointed Ears

The bull terrier has small triangular bat-like ears placed close together. They should be stiffly erect and point straight upwards. The inside of the ears are made from pink handmade paper and their outside matches the terrier's fur colouring, one in white handmade paper and the other in brown.

Long, Slender Ears

The rabbit has long, oval-shaped ears positioned directly behind its head. Fold each ear in half, with the beige layer on top. Use a little PVA adhesive to attach them onto the rabbit's head, folded edges side by side, making sure their beige inner ear is facing outwards and the tips of the ears point towards the back-end.

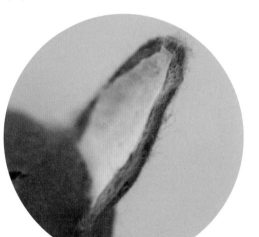

Folded Ears

The Labrador has small, oval-shaped ears. After gluing the ears onto the back of the head, fold or bend them up at their base and then at the halfway point, fold the tip of each ear down, so that they hang close to the head and are set slightly above the eyes.

Floppy Ears

The dachshund has broad, moderate length, well-rounded ears set high and not too far forward on the head. Attach the ears onto the top of the head, with their inner ear facing towards the side so that they drape down on either side.

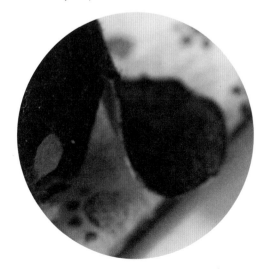

Fabulous Faces

The most important part of making a pebble pet is in creating its adorable face. Try to take your time and use a steady hand when adding on a pet's facial details. Study their real life counterparts or photographs of them to see where the eyes, nose and mouth are in relationship to each other. Try not to make any of your pets' eyes too large, as oversized eyes will make them look like a cartoon character. Follow the instructions below to create the basic facial details.

Fast Asleep

Use a grey brush-tip pen, which has a very soft touch to control, to draw on an animal's sleeping eyes in the shape of a semicircle at a point not quite halfway to the top of the head. You can use the same pen to create the pet's nose by drawing a U on the tip of the face and suggest the mouth by extending a line down from its bottom slightly to create an upside down Y.

Open Wide

To create opened eyes, use a teardrop punch to create two teardrops from black craft paper. Using a drop of PVA adhesive, attach them on to the face in the desired position, while making sure they are level and balanced in relation to the rest of the face.

Bright Eyes

For shiny, bold eyes use white acrylic paint to add a tiny dot of white to each of the eyes, creating a reflection of light. When the paint is dry, cover the eyes with a layer of clear nail varnish so that they become shiny and bold.

Healthy Nose and Tongue

Cut a small oval from a piece of pink handmade paper for a pet's tongue and glue it into place. Apply a layer of clear nail varnish to the nose and tongue to add shine for a healthy look.

The Cat's Whiskers

Whiskers add a realistic touch to your pebble pets and are so easy to create; simply follow these easy instructions.

YOU WILL NEED:
- beading thread or clear nylon fishing line
- PVA adhesive
- scissors

1 Cut three strands of beading thread or clear nylon fishing line to approximately the same length as the width of the pet's body. Place them horizontally on your working surface.

2 Using tiny drops of PVA adhesive, attach the strands together at their middle point. When the adhesive is dry, cut the strands in half vertically at their glued area to make a set of whiskers.

3 Finally, using a drop of PVA adhesive, attach the whiskers in place on either side of the pet's nose.

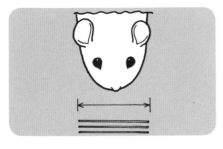

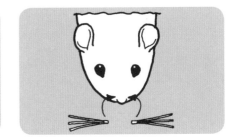

Love that Face!

By following the step-by-step instructions for each project and varying the shape of the eyes, detail of the mouth and angle of the head, you can create a wide range of irresistible and life-like expressions for your pebble pets.

Sleeping Beauty

To show your pebble pet in the land of dreams, simply draw on two semicircles for the eyes and choose a pebble that is roughly in the shape of an orange segment to resemble the pet curled in snugly on itself.

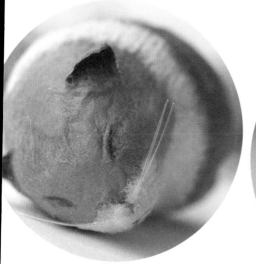

Wide-Eyed Wonder
Who could resist this adorable face? The Boston terrier's large, round eyes are set wide apart and are alert with a gentle expression. A circular-shaped paper punch is used to create the eyes and a tiny dot of white acrylic paint is painted into each one before they are coated with a layer of clear nail varnish for the perfect shine.

Groomed to Perfection
This gorgeous grooming pose is created by slightly angling the Siamese's head pebble when attaching it to the body and creating a dark pink tongue from handmade paper. The closed eyes, drawn on as semicircles with a black brush-tip pen and protruding whiskers add to the effect.

PERFECT PETS

There is something undeniably magical about transforming a single pebble into an adorable pet to treasure. In this section, you will discover how to build up your pet's fur colouring, ears, nose and tail to create a wonderful range of animals, from cute chipmunks and hamsters to rabbits and pigs that are full of character and charm. You won't be able to resist trying out the variation projects and creating a range of enchanting little accessories that will guarantee a happy pet!

These perfect pets each require a kidney bean-shaped pebble for their foundation. Look at both ends of your pebble and pick the one you think is best suited for the pet's face. If the pebble tapers, then use the

 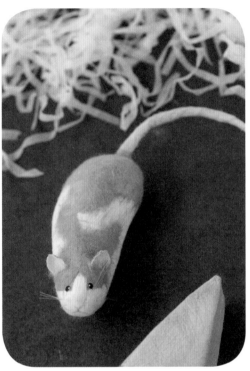 

slightly smaller end, or if both ends are the same, then select the smoothest one. Feel free to experiment with your pebble shape, for example by choosing a pebble that is twisted slightly or has one end that points up or down. The more interesting the pebble's appearance, then the more character your finished pet will have.

You may find it helpful to start with the Guinea Pigs chapter (see pages 26–31) and work through it with care, as it provides full step-by-step instructions to guide you in the basic procedures required to make a pebble pet. Remember that a little patience at this stage in making your pebble pet will enable you to reap great rewards later on when you attempt something more ambitious.

Guinea Pigs

Bubble & Squeak

Guinea pigs are small, burrowing rodents that have enjoyed widespread popularity as household pets since their introduction by European traders in the 16th century. They are widely recognized for their compact bodies, short ears and legs and long claws, and their coat colours include white, brown, yellow and black. The most common breeds are the English shorthair, which has a short, smooth coat, and the Abyssinian, whose coat is ruffled with cowlicks. Guinea pigs are vegetarian and their diet consists mainly of hay, grain and vegetables.

Due to their docile nature, responsiveness to handling and the relative ease of caring for them, guinea pigs make popular pets. They are inexpensive, thrive in groups of two or more and can be kept in cages either indoors or outdoors. Guinea pigs have poor sight, but well-developed senses of hearing, smell and touch. While they can jump over small obstacles, they cannot climb and are not particularly agile. They startle very easily and will either freeze in place for long periods or run for cover with quick, darting motions when they sense danger. Guinea pigs typically live an average of four to five years, but some can live for a maximum of eight years.

Pet Profile

Bubble is a gentle tricolour shorthaired guinea pig who is a proud mother to this beautiful little pup, named Squeak. Most pups will suckle for four to five weeks but Squeak is showing his adventurous streak and has already started to nibble on his mother's food. Squeak will stay with Bubble until he is six weeks old, when he will be fully weaned and ready to leave his mother's side to go to a new home.

Squeak is on his best behaviour as his mother teaches him what he can eat, chew and play with. Bubble is a firm teacher and may give her pup a little nip or kick if he fails to respond quickly to her.

Bubble

Pebble focus: you will need one kidney bean-shaped pebble, a little pointed at one end and large and rounded at the other. It should be approximately the same size as a duck's egg and should sit comfortably in the palm of your hand (see page 6).

1 To make the ears, use a pencil, ruler and scissors to mark, measure and cut out three 2 x 3cm (¾ x 1⅛in) rectangles: one each in brown and pink handmade paper and white craft paper. Following the instructions on page 20 and using the ear template below, make up the ears using pink handmade paper for the inner ear colouring. Set the ears aside.

Guinea pig ear template

2 **To make the body**, use the glue mix to cover the pebble completely with pieces of white handmade paper. When the glue is dry, use a pencil to lightly mark the line of the spine and ears, working from the top of the head to the back-end.

3 Tear out two ovals from brown handmade paper. The ovals should be of an adequate size to fill the spaces between the top of the head and cheek on either side.

4 Apply glue mix to each oval, working it evenly from the centre of the paper out towards and over the torn edges.

5 Carefully attach the ovals onto the face to fill the spaces between the top of the head and the cheeks, covering up the ear-line in the process.

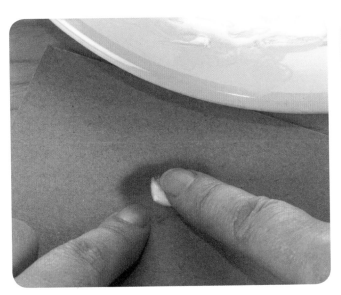

6 Use the glue mix to cover the remainder of the top of the body to the rump and back-end with pieces of black and brown handmade paper in a pattern of your choice.

7 **Attach the ears** on top of the head using a little PVA adhesive. The pink inner ear should face towards the front of the guinea pig with the ear-line lying beneath. Use small pieces of brown handmade paper to hide the join between the ears and forehead.

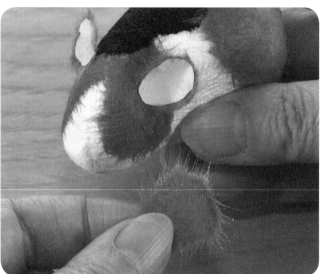

8 When the PVA adhesive is dry, gently lift the ears away from the head to make them stand up slightly. Fold the tip of each ear down a little to suggest that the ears are drooping.

9 **To mark the nose and mouth**, apply a little glue mix to the nose and mouth area, then attach small pieces of pink facial tissue over the glued area. When the glue is dry, use a grey brush-tip pen to draw on a small U for the guinea pig's nose and an upside down Y for its mouth.

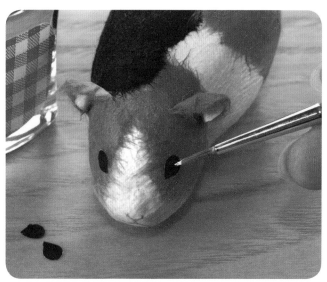

Giving Bubble drooping ears, shiny eyes and drawing on an upside down Y for her mouth forms a contented expression which can be reflected on her pup's face.

10 **To make the eyes**, use a teardrop punch to create two teardrops from black craft paper. Using a drop of PVA adhesive, attach them onto the face in the desired position and add a tiny dot of white acrylic paint to each eye. When the paint is dry, cover the eyes with a layer of clear nail varnish to make them shiny and bold.

Squeak

This adorable guinea pig pup is created using the same materials and techniques as for the mother guinea pig, but of course, everything is on a smaller scale. For this variation, use a small pebble in a similar shape but about half the size of that used for the mother.

Differentiate the design slightly from the mother guinea pig by varying the pattern of the handmade coloured paper. Here we have used black handmade paper torn into an oval shape to cover one eye and created one of the ears with black handmade paper to give Squeak his own characteristics. Working on a much smaller scale can result in mistakes being made, so be careful and patient during the early stages of the pup's construction.

Rabbits

Peaches & Furby

Rabbits are docile, intelligent, inquisitive and extremely social creatures that have become extremely popular as domestic pets. The lop-eared rabbit is the oldest known breed of domestic rabbit and can be traced as far back as 1700CE. The Dutch rabbit is another popular breed that was first bred in the Netherlands and brought to England in 1864. Visually striking, its most dominant characteristic is the formal attire of its markings with a broad band of white fur around the front part of its body.

With their relative ease of care and wide range of breeds, colours and coat types, rabbits have become a popular pet worldwide. A pet rabbit's diet typically consists of unlimited hay, a small amount of pellets and a small portion of fresh vegetables. They can be kept outside in a suitable hutch or as house rabbits if given an indoor pen or cage and a safe place to exercise. To stimulate a pet rabbit, it is important to equip the pen with enrichment activities such as shelves, tunnels, balls and other toys, and to provide an area to allow them to exercise sufficiently.

Pet Profile

Peaches, a placid lop-eared rabbit, and Furby, her more energetic Dutch rabbit companion, were both bought from a local pet shop when they were eight weeks old. They are both happy being handled, love each other's company and adore running around in their fenced-in garden playground.

Peaches and Furby love exploring their play area. Peaches is happily bounding on the grass, while Furby is munching on a favourite titbit, a little piece of carrot. Instructions on how to make the carrot can be found on page 37.

Peaches

YOU WILL NEED:

- two A5 (21 x 15cm/8¼ x 5¾in) rectangles of handmade paper: one each in light brown and pink for the body and ears
- two A5 (21 x 15cm/8¼ x 5¾in) rectangles of craft paper: one each in black and white for the ears and eyes
- one 3cm (1⅛in) length of 24-gauge white covered florists' wire for the tail
- teardrop punch
- basic tool kit (see pages 12–13)

Pebble focus: you will need one egg-shaped pebble. It should be approximately the same size as a hen's egg and should sit comfortably in the palm of your hand.

1 To make the ears, use a pencil, ruler and scissors to mark, measure and cut out three 3.5cm (1⅜in) squares: one each in light brown and pink handmade paper and white craft paper. Following the instructions on page 20 and using the ear template below, make up the ears using pink handmade paper for the inner ear colouring. Set the ears aside.

2 To make the tail, wrap small amounts of cotton wool around one end of the florists' wire to create a pointed tail-like shape that is 1cm (⅜in) in length and 0.8cm (⁵⁄₁₆in) in width.

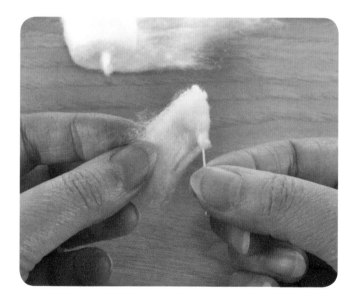

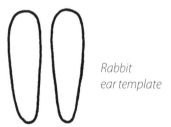

Rabbit ear template

3 Tear out a piece of brown handmade paper that is slightly larger than the tail and smear glue mix all over the paper. Wrap the paper around the tail, so that its sides overlap a little, being careful to maintain the tail's shape. Set the tail aside.

4 **To make the body**, use the glue mix to completely cover the pebble with pieces of light brown handmade paper. When the glue is dry, use a pencil to lightly mark the line of the ears.

5 **To attach the ears**, firstly fold the ears in half lengthways with their pink side on top. Attach the ears on top of the head using a little PVA adhesive, with the pink inner ear facing towards the front of the rabbit, the ear-line lying beneath and ensuring the ears drape down. Use small pieces of light brown handmade paper to hide the join between the ears and head.

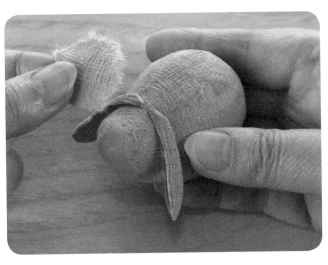

The tail is simply made by wrapping cotton wool around a piece of florists' wire and covering with handmade paper. If you would prefer more of a pompom-shaped tail, simply attach a small ball of white cotton wool with a little PVA adhesive.

6 **To attach the tail**, use a little PVA adhesive to glue the wired end onto the underside of the body's back-end. Use a small piece of light brown handmade paper to hide the join between the tail and body.

7 **To make the face**, use a grey brush-tip pen to draw on a small U for the rabbit's nose and an upside down Y for its mouth.

8 **To make the eyes**, use a teardrop punch to create two teardrops from black craft paper. Using a drop of PVA adhesive, attach them onto the face in the desired position and add a tiny dot of white acrylic paint to each eye. When the paint is dry, cover the eyes with a layer of clear nail varnish.

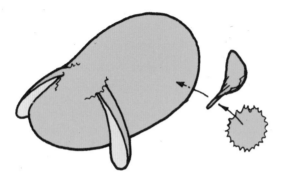

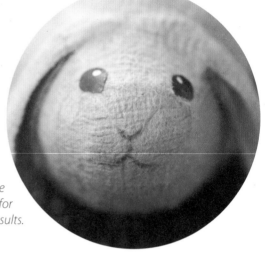

The long lop ears elegantly frame the rabbit's gentle expression for simply adorable results.

Furby

This striking black and white Dutch rabbit is created using a similar sized pebble and the same techniques as for Peaches. You will need two A5 (21 x 15cm/8¼ x 5¾in) rectangles of craft paper: one each in black and white to cover the ears, eyes and body.

Use white handmade paper to completely cover the pebble, then add pieces of black handmade paper to the rabbit's head, cheeks, rump and underside, being careful to leave the white paper area of its nose and a broad band around the middle clear. Make the tail in black and attach small pieces of pink facial tissue over the nose and mouth area. For the ears, use pieces of black (outer ear) and beige (inner ear) handmade papers and white craft paper. See page 21 for details on how to attach the ears to the rabbit's head.

Making Up the Carrot

What better way to treat your rabbit than by tempting him with a carrot to nibble on? It is so simple to create and makes the perfect healthy snack for your furry friend.

YOU WILL NEED:

- two A5 (21 x 15cm/8¼ x 5¾in) rectangles of handmade paper: one each in bright orange and dark green for the carrot and leaves
- three 4cm (1½in) lengths of 24-gauge white covered florists' wire
- basic tool kit (see pages 12–13)

1 **To make a leaf**, use a pencil, ruler and scissors to mark, measure and cut out a 1 x 5cm (⅜ x 2in) rectangle of dark green handmade paper. Place the paper sideways on. Fold and unfold it in half from side to side and top to bottom. Cut off and discard the upper left-hand quarter of paper. Cut a tiny fringe along the right-hand half's top edge making a toothbrush-like shape, being careful not to cut right through to the bottom edge.

2 Smear glue mix all over the paper's lower half. Place a length of florists' wire on top of the paper's fringed right-hand side. Slant the paper at a slight angle and wind it spirally down, covering the wire by rotating it.

3 Continue winding the paper to the end of the wire. Set the leaf aside. Repeat steps 1 to 3 with the remaining two lengths of florists' wire.

4 **To make the root**, mould a piece of modelling clay into a 1 x 4cm (⅜ x 1½in) root-like shape that is rounded at one end and tapers towards a blunt, rounded tip. Using a modelling spatula, make a hole into the root's rounded end. Let the clay dry.

5 Using the glue mix, cover the root completely with pieces of bright orange handmade paper. Poke the stalk end of each leaf through the paper and into the root's hole. Secure them in place with a drop of PVA adhesive.

6 When the adhesive/glue is dry, use a grey brush-tip pen to draw on the carrot's wavy markings.

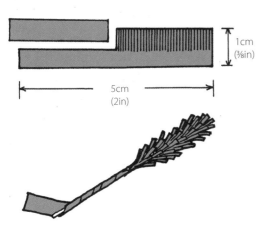

1cm
(⅜in)

5cm
(2in)

Rat

Rex

Rats are medium sized, long-tailed rodents, typically distinguished from mice by their size. Specially bred rats have been kept as pets since the late 19th century. Typically, pet rats are variants of the brown rat species, but black rats and giant pouched rats can also be kept. They exhibit a variety of coat types, ranging from long, fine hair to semi-hairless and bare skin. Rats are omnivores and benefit from a diet consisting of a mix of wholesome foods and animal proteins. Domestic rats differ from wild rats in many ways. They are calmer and less likely to bite, can tolerate greater crowding, are likely to produce more offspring, and can become very tame and attached to their owners. They make playful, sensitive pets and can be taught to come by name and perform a variety of simple tricks. It is better to keep rats in wire-walled cages rather than glass or plastic tanks, as they love to climb. Domestic rats do tend to get bored easily and require plenty of games and puzzles to keep them entertained. They are nocturnal creatures and the average lifespan of a domestic rat is two to three years.

Pet Profile

Rex is an extremely alert and active rat who responds to his name and loves to be picked up and handled. He is very clean and constantly preens himself to look his best at all times. Rex is the Houdini of the rat world and loves to escape through the wires of his cage and squeeze under doors in the search for food.

Rex loves to escape from his cage to search for snacks. Here, he has snuck away to enjoy a tasty piece of cheese (see page 42 for making up instructions).

Rex

YOU WILL NEED:

- three A5 (21 x 15cm/8¼ x 5¾in) rectangles of handmade paper: one each in grey, pink and white for the body, ears and tail
- two A5 (21 x 15cm/8¼ x 5¾in) rectangles of craft paper: one each in black and white for the ears and eyes
- one 8cm (3⅛in) length of 24-gauge white covered florists' wire for the tail
- one pink facial tissue
- circle punch
- basic tool kit (see pages 12–13)

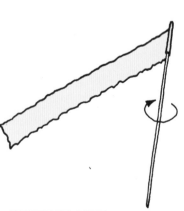

Pebble focus: you will need one stretched bean-shaped pebble that is slightly curved to one side, giving the rat an interesting pose. The pebble should sit comfortably in the palm of your hand.

1 To make the ears, use a pencil, ruler and scissors to mark, measure and cut out three 1.5 x 3cm (⅝ x 1⅛in) rectangles: one each in grey and pink handmade paper and white craft paper. Following the instructions on page 20 and using the ear template below, make up the ears using pink handmade paper for the inner ear colouring. Set the ears aside.

 Rat ear template

2 To make the tail, use a pencil, ruler and scissors to mark, measure and cut out a 1 x 10cm (⅜ x 4in) rectangle of pink handmade paper. Smear glue mix all over the paper. Place the florists' wire on top of the paper's right-hand side.

3 Slant the paper at a slight angle and wind it spirally down, covering the wire by rotating it. Continue to the end of the wire. Set the tail aside.

The tail gives your rat balance and will add to its character. Give the tail a pronounced curve by bending it to one side to give your rat a natural pose.

4 **To make the body**, use the glue mix to completely cover the pebble with pieces of white handmade paper. When the glue is dry, use a pencil to lightly mark the line of the spine and ears, working from the top of the head to the back-end.

5 **For the facial details**, tear out two small wedge-like shapes from grey handmade paper that are large enough to cover the front of the face and ear-line. Attach them onto the front of the face to suggest the letter W. The rat's eyes will be placed into the points of the W at a later stage.

6 **Attach the ears** on top of the head using a little PVA adhesive. The pink inner ear should face towards the front of the rat with the ear-line lying beneath. Use small pieces of grey handmade paper to hide the join between the ears and head. When the PVA adhesive is dry, gently lift the ears away from the head to make them stand up slightly.

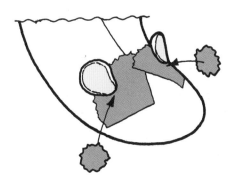

7 Apply a little glue mix to the nose and mouth area and attach small pieces of pink facial tissue over the glued area. When the glue is dry, use a grey brush-tip pen to draw on a small U for the rat's nose and an upside down Y for its mouth.

8 **To make the eyes**, use a circle punch to create two circles from black craft paper. Using a drop of PVA adhesive, attach them onto the face in the desired position and add a tiny dot of white acrylic paint to each eye. When the paint is dry, cover the eyes with a layer of clear nail varnish.

9 Using the glue mix, cover the remainder of the top of the body with small pieces of grey handmade paper and most of the back-end with larger pieces.

10 **To attach the tail**, bend one end over slightly. Using a little PVA adhesive, attach the tail via its bent end onto the body's back-end.

11 Use a small piece of grey handmade paper to hide the join between the tail and body. When the adhesive is dry, gently curve the tail into the desired shape.

12 **To add the whiskers**, follow the instructions on page 23 using beading thread or clear nylon fishing line. Attach the whiskers in place on either side of the rat's nose using a drop of PVA adhesive.

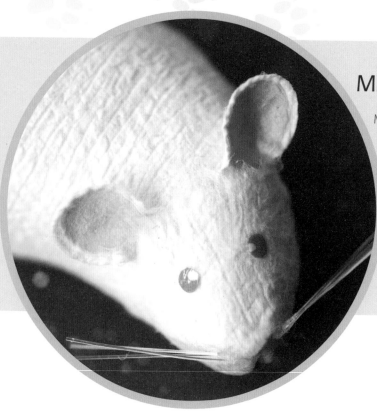

Mint

Mint is a little white mouse who enjoys being picked up and placed on the palm of her owner's hand, where she can nibble on a sunflower seed or two. She is created using the same techniques as for the rat (pages 40–41) using a similar-shaped, but smaller-sized pebble.

Use white handmade paper to completely cover the pebble. For the ears, use pieces of white handmade paper for the outer ear, pink handmade paper for the inner ear and white craft paper. Use pink handmade paper for the tail and a pink facial tissue for the nose and mouth. The eyes are punched from pink craft paper.

Making Up the Cheese

This tasty chunk of Edam is sure to tempt any rodent on the search for food! It is easy to create using modelling clay as the base and covering with handmade paper for realistic results.

YOU WILL NEED:

• two A5 (21 x 15cm/8¼ x 5¾in) rectangles of handmade paper: one each in red and yellow for the cheese and wax coating
• basic tool kit (see pages 12–13)

1 Mould a piece of modelling clay into a triangle shape, approximately the same size as a hen's egg. Let the clay dry.

2 Using the glue mix, cover the triangle completely with pieces of yellow handmade paper.

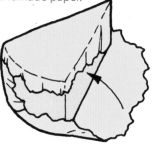

3 **For the wax coating**, cut out a rectangle from red handmade paper. This should be of a sufficient size to cover the triangle's curved surface. Use the glue mix to attach it on.

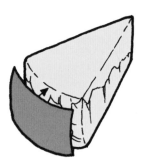

Hamsters

Ginger & Biscuit

Hamsters are fun-loving rodents that have become recently established as popular family pets. The best-known species is the Syrian or golden hamster. Characteristically plump in appearance, hamsters are known for their flexible bodies, small ears, short tails and stocky legs. Their thick, silky fur can be long or short and varies in colour, some of the most common coats being cream, golden brown, black, grey, yellow or white. Hamsters are omnivorous and are well known for storing food away in their cheek pouches. Their diet consists mostly of grains but can also include fresh fruit, carrots and green leaves. They are clean, easy to care for and can be kept in cages or glass tanks.

Hamsters are surprisingly good climbers and are skilled at digging chambers for nesting and food storage. Like all pets, they need exercise and entertainment to maintain their physical and mental wellbeing and they should be provided with a wheel in the cage or a plastic ball for exploring outside the cage. Hamsters are also gnawers and must be supplied with appropriate materials for doing so. Syrian hamsters typically live no more than two to three years in captivity.

Pet Profile

Ginger and Biscuit are small Syrian hamsters with big personalities. When they are not entertaining themselves with their acrobatic tricks, racing each other across the floor in their plastic exercise balls or trying to gnaw their way out of their cage, they enjoy the simple pleasure of curling up into a ball for a satisfying sleep.

These two hamsters are very content companions. Here, Ginger is protectively guarding Biscuit as she sleeps, busily munching on the many seeds he stores in his bulging cheek pouches.

Ginger

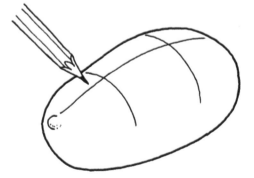

YOU WILL NEED:

- five A5 (21 x 15cm/8¼ x 5¾in) rectangles of handmade paper: one each in brown, cream, grey, orange and white for the body and tail
- two A5 (21 x 15cm/8¼ x 5¾in) rectangles of craft paper: one each in black and white for the ears and eyes
- one pink facial tissue
- teardrop punch
- basic tool kit (see pages 12–13)

Pebble focus: you will need one broad bean-shaped pebble, a little pointed at one end. It should be approximately the same size as a hen's egg and should sit comfortably in the palm of your hand.

1 **To make the ears,** use a pencil, ruler and scissors to mark, measure and cut out three 2 x 3cm (¾ x 1⅛in) rectangles: one each in brown and grey handmade paper and white craft paper. Following the instructions on page 20 and using the ear template below, make up the ears using grey handmade paper for the inner ear colouring. Set the ears aside.

Hamster ear template

2 **To make the tail,** tear out a fingertip-sized circle from white handmade paper. Apply a little glue mix to the paper and roll the paper to mould it into a tiny tail that is approximately the size of a long grain of rice. Cover it with a fingertip-sized piece of pink facial tissue and set the tail aside.

3 **To make the body,** add a small knob of modelling clay to the pebble's pointed end to suggest the hamster's nose. Let the clay dry. Use the glue mix to cover the pebble and clay completely with pieces of white handmade paper. When the glue is dry, use a pencil to lightly mark the line of the spine, ears and rump, working from the nose to the back-end.

4 Starting from the nose and finishing slightly past the ear-line, cover the top of the body by gluing on pieces of cream handmade paper, then add pieces of orange handmade paper to suggest the coat pattern.

5 Apply a little glue mix to the nose and mouth area. Attach small pieces of pink facial tissue over the glued area. When the glue is dry, use a grey brush-tip pen to draw on a small U for the hamster's nose and an upside down Y for its mouth.

6 **Attach the ears** on top of the head using a little PVA adhesive. The grey inner ear should face towards the front of the hamster with the ear-line lying beneath. Use small pieces of brown handmade paper to suggest the face's graduational colouring and to hide the join between the ears and head. When the adhesive is dry, gently lift the ears away from the body to make them stand up slightly.

7 Using a little PVA adhesive, attach the tail onto the underside of the body's back-end. Use a small piece of white handmade paper to hide the join between the tail and body.

8 Using the glue mix, cover the remainder of the top of the body with pieces of orange and brown handmade paper, being careful to leave the white paper areas of the chest, part of the sides and abdomen clear.

9 **To make the eyes**, use a teardrop punch to create two teardrops from black craft paper. Using a drop of PVA adhesive, attach them onto the face in the desired position and add a tiny dot of white acrylic paint to each eye. When the paint is dry, cover the eyes with a layer of clear nail varnish.

10 **To make the whiskers**, follow the instructions on page 23 using beading thread or clear nylon fishing line. Attach the whiskers in place on either side of the hamster's nose using a drop of PVA adhesive.

Ginger's wide-eyed look is created using a teardrop punch. A layer of clear nail varnish is added for extra shine. To vary the look and create a sleeping pose, draw a simple semicircle shape using a grey brush-tip pen, as we have done with Biscuit below.

Biscuit

This cute cinnamon coloured hamster is created using the same techniques as for the golden hamster. For this variation, use a pebble the same size as above, roughly in the shape of an orange segment and slightly rounded at one end.

For the ears, use pieces of cinnamon handmade paper for the outer ear and grey handmade paper for the inner ear. Use pink facial tissue for the tail and use cinnamon and white handmade papers for the body, leaving a white band across its middle as shown. To create the sleeping pose, draw closed eyes using a grey brush-tip pen and glue the ears and whiskers flat towards the body.

Chipmunks

Cino & Mocha

Chipmunks can be likened to small stripy squirrels and they originate predominantly from North America. The most widespread and smallest species is the least chipmunk, which is recognizable by the dark stripes that adorn its face and body, grey and red-brown coats and orange-brown tails. As a species, chipmunks have only recently been domesticated, so should still be thought of as semi-wild. They have very distinct personalities; some can be independent, distant and nervous, whilst others display intelligence and can be quickly tamed.

Chipmunks are full of energy and need a lot of space to play and exercise in. They can be kept in an indoor aviary or large nest box, and should be provided with sufficient branches and shelves to run around on and hiding places to nest in. Domestic chipmunks kept indoors will not hibernate, although those kept outside in an aviary are very likely to hibernate throughout the winter. Their diet should consist mainly of unsalted nuts, seeds and grains, and fresh foods such as grapes and pieces of apple. The average life expectancy for a male is four to five years in captivity; females, however, can live for up to nine years.

Pet Profile

Cino and Mocha are both highly energetic and love to perform acrobatic tricks on the tree branches that they have in their cage. They store more food than they actually eat and as a treat, they enjoy nuts in their shells. The shells allow them to wear down their continuously growing teeth while at the same time preventing boredom.

When they finally tire themselves out, Cino and Mocha love nothing more than to sit down on a branch to rest and watch the world go by.

Cino

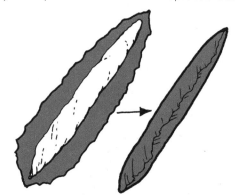

YOU WILL NEED:

- three A5 (21 x 15cm/8¼ x 5¾in) rectangles of handmade paper: one each in brown, mustard yellow and white for the body, ears and tail
- two A5 (21 x 15cm/8¼ x 5¾in) rectangles of craft paper: one each in black and white for the ears and eyes
- one 5cm (2in) length of 24-gauge white covered florists' wire for the tail
- teardrop punch
- basic tool kit (see pages 12–13)

Pebble focus: you will need one round ended triangular-shaped pebble that will sit up without wobbling.

1 To make the ears, use a pencil, ruler and scissors to mark, measure and cut out three 1 x 2cm (³⁄₈ x ¾in) rectangles: two from brown handmade paper and one from white craft paper. Following the instructions on page 20 and using the ear template below, make up the ears using brown handmade paper for the inner and outer ear colouring. Set the ears aside.

○ ○ *Chipmunk ear template*

2 To make the tail, wrap small amounts of cotton wool around the florists' wire, making a long French bean-like shape that is approximately 5mm (³⁄₁₆in) in diameter.

3 Tear out a paddle-like shape from brown handmade paper, 1.5 x 6cm (⁵⁄₈ x 2³⁄₈in) in size. Smear glue mix all over the paper. Wrap the paper around the wire and cotton wool, so that its sides overlap a little and shape one end slightly into a point to create the tail's tip. Set the tail aside.

4 To make the body, add a small amount of modelling clay to the tip of the pebble's top point to suggest the chipmunk's pointed face. Let the clay dry. Using the glue mix, cover the pebble and clay completely with pieces of white handmade paper.

5 When the glue is dry, use a pencil to lightly mark the line of the spine and ears, working from the top of the head to the back-end.

6 Using the glue mix, cover the sides of the face and body with pieces of mustard yellow handmade paper from the cheek to the back-end.

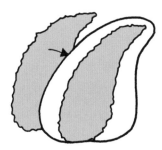

7 **Attach the ears** on the top of the head using a little PVA adhesive. The brown inner ear should face towards the front of the chipmunk with the ear-line lying beneath. Use small pieces of mustard yellow handmade paper to hide the join between the ears and head. When the adhesive is dry, gently lift the ears away from the head to make them stand up and alert.

8 **To make the chipmunk's stripes**, use a pencil and ruler to mark and measure out two rectangles from brown handmade paper, calculating the size by multiplying 1cm (³⁄₈in) by the length of the body (from the ears to the back-end). Tear them out, then carefully tear each one in half lengthways to make four narrow strips.

9 Use a glue stick to attach the strips onto the back, working from the ears to the back-end and either side of the line of the spine. Be careful to leave a small strip of white handmade paper in-between the strips of paper to suggest the chipmunk's striped markings.

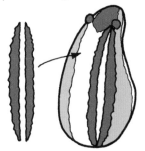

10 Using a little PVA adhesive, attach the non-pointed end of the tail onto the underside of the body's back-end. Use a small piece of white handmade paper to hide the join between the tail and body. When the adhesive is dry, gently curve the tail into the desired shape.

11 **To make the face**, tear out a teardrop-shaped piece from brown handmade paper, the size of which should fill the space between the nose and forehead. Use the glue mix to attach it onto the relevant place.

12 **To make the eyes**, use a teardrop punch to create two teardrops from black craft paper. Using a drop of PVA adhesive, attach them onto the face in the desired position and add a tiny dot of white acrylic paint to each eye. When the paint is dry, cover the eyes with a layer of clear nail varnish.

13 Using a grey brush-tip pen, draw on a small U for the chipmunk's nose, an upside down Y for its mouth, and stripes above and below each eye.

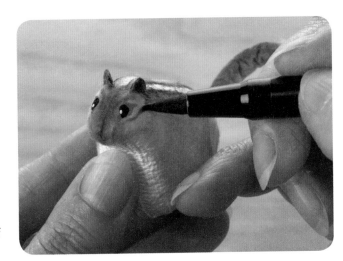

Mocha

Mocha is a mischievous eastern chipmunk, created using the same techniques as for Cino, using brown, dark brown and white handmade papers to create the appearance of darker fur. For this variation, use a long bean-shaped pebble that has one end looking upwards to resemble the typical attentive chipmunk pose.

Pig & Piglets

Rosie & Her Piglets

Pot-bellied and dwarf breeds of pigs have become popular house pets. Domestic farmyard pigs can also be kept as house pets, however they usually need to be moved into an outdoor pen as they grow larger, due to their destructive tendencies. Pigs are complex animals; typically they display naturally curious and playful characteristics and are able to be readily trained. As pets, they can be rewarding and entertaining; however they require an owner who understands their needs and is familiar with their behaviour, especially when keeping them as piglets. Without appropriate stimulation, they can become easily bored and possibly destructive. Pigs will eat just about anything, although their diets should be restricted to grains, such as wheat, barley, or oats, and fruit and vegetables to facilitate good digestion. They can be unrelenting in their quest for food and can even learn to open cupboards and fridge doors in search of a snack! Pigs also can be territorial and strive to be dominant. They need to be taught to respect their owners: positive reinforcement, consistent rules and praise for good behaviour produce a well-mannered animal. Pigs will live an average of 12–18 years.

Pet Profile

Rosie and her piglets belong to a breed of pig known as the British lop, one of the most endangered of all native pig species. Extremely hardy, they can be kept outdoors all year round. Rosie is an excellent mother with a very docile nature and she prides herself on taking good care of her piglets.

Here, Rosie and her piglets are busy exploring their surroundings on a quest to find food. This straw bedding is perfect for them to burrow under when they feel cold.

Rosie

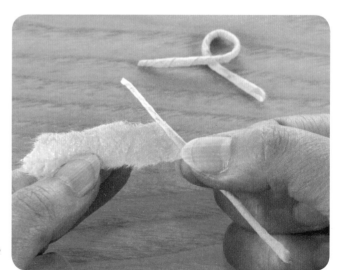

YOU WILL NEED:

- two A5 (21 x 15cm/8¼ x 5¾in) rectangles of handmade paper: one each in light pink and dark pink for the body, ears and tail
- two A5 (21 x 15cm/8¼ x 5¾in) rectangles of craft paper: one each in black and white for the ears and eyes
- one 7cm (2¾in) length of 24-gauge white covered florists' wire for the tail
- circle punch
- basic tool kit (see pages 12–13)

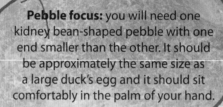

Pebble focus: you will need one kidney bean-shaped pebble with one end smaller than the other. It should be approximately the same size as a large duck's egg and it should sit comfortably in the palm of your hand.

1 To make the ears, use a pencil, ruler and scissors to mark, measure and cut out three 3.5 x 4.5cm (1⅜ x 1¾in) rectangles: two from light pink handmade paper and one from white craft paper. Following the instructions on page 20 and using the ear template below, make up the ears using light pink handmade paper for the inner and outer ear colouring. Set the ears aside.

Pig ear template

2 To make the tail, use a pencil and ruler to mark and measure out a 1 x 10cm (⅜ x 4in) rectangle of light pink handmade paper. Tear out and smear glue mix all over it. Place the florists' wire on top of the paper's right-hand side.

3 Slant the paper at a slight angle and wind it spirally down, covering the wire by rotating it. Continue to the end of the wire. When the glue is dry, twist the paper covered wire into a loose curl. Set the tail aside.

4 **To make the body and snout**, add a small amount of modelling clay to the smaller end of the pebble. Using a modelling spatula, mould the clay into the shape of an upside-down heart to suggest the pig's snout. Let the clay dry. Using the glue mix, cover the pebble and clay completely with pieces of light pink handmade paper.

7 Use small pieces of light pink handmade paper to hide the join between the ears and head. When the adhesive is dry, bend each ear towards the snout. Give the tips of the ears a little pinch to make them floppy-like in appearance.

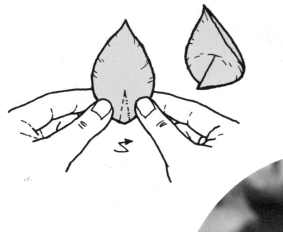

8 Using a little PVA adhesive, attach one end of the tail onto the body's back-end. Use a small piece of light pink handmade paper to hide the join between the tail and body.

5 When the glue is dry, use a pencil to lightly mark the line of the spine and ears, working from the snout to the back-end.

6 **To attach the ears**, make a small pleat in the bottom edge of each ear to make them cup-like in appearance. Using a little PVA adhesive, attach the ears on the top of the head with their cupped side facing towards the front of the pig and the ear-line lying beneath.

9 Using the glue mix, cover the remainder of the top of the body with pieces of dark pink handmade paper, making sure that no pencil lines show through.

10 **To make the eyes, nostrils and mouth**, use a circle punch to create two circles from black craft paper for the eyes. Using a drop of PVA adhesive, attach them onto the face in the desired position. Using a grey brush-tip pen, draw two teardrop-shaped nostrils onto the pig's snout and a stretched out W for its mouth.

One of the most recognizable features of the pig is its pink curly tail. Make this as curly as you like by twisting the paper-covered florists' wire into a loose spiral before attaching it onto the body.

The Piglets

The adorable and very energetic little piglets are created using the same techniques and similar materials as for their mother (see pages 54–55), however they are obviously smaller in proportion.

For a piglet's foundation, use a kidney bean-shaped pebble, similar in size to a quail's egg and for its tail, you will need a 3cm (1⅛in) length of 24-gauge white covered florists' wire. To make up the ears in proportion to their bodies, follow the instructions on pages 54–55, using the ear template below.

Piglet ear template

Bruno

This very hardy, white-banded British saddleback is also created using exactly the same techniques as for the British lop (see pages 54–55). For this variation, use a plump kidney bean-shaped pebble to suggest the pig's stout appearance.

Use slate or graphite grey and pink coloured handmade papers for the pig's body, making sure to leave a broad pink band across its saddle. For the ears inside colouring and snout, use beige or light brown coloured handmade paper.

DESIRABLE DOGS

Since they became domesticated, loyalty and friendship have characterized the relationship between dogs and their owners. Using this section, you can create a wide variety of dog breeds to keep with you at all times as loyal and adorable companions. A range of well-known breeds has been selected, from the gorgeous black and tan dachshund to the muscular Shiba Inu. As it is difficult to portray long legged or bushy long fur breeds by means of our pebble technique, we have chosen to depict breeds that are short-legged or have shown them sitting or lying down in a variety of realistic poses.

Our canine friends are all made up by attaching together two pebbles, using a larger interestingly shaped pebble for the body and a smaller, rounder pebble for the head. Your modelling skills will move on as you discover the simple method of joining two pebbles together and cleverly hiding joins between the head

pebble and the body pebble with an attractive collar. By altering the size of the pebbles, you can make either puppies or adults, and by using combinations of different colours and types of handmade paper, the dog breeds you can create can be extended.

To get to grips with the two-pebble technique, you may wish to begin with the Bull Terrier chapter (see page 60–65), which provides full step-by-step instructions to guide you through how to join your pebbles and attach the collar of your choice (see pages 96–98). You can also create a stunning array of accessories, from cosy cushions and blankets to tasty bones and bouncing balls, following the simple making up instructions on pages 98–101. Feel free to adapt any project to suit your requirements, or simply experiment to develop your own approaches and ideas to create the perfect pooch pal for you.

Bull Terrier

Henry

The bull terrier, also known as the English bull terrier, was developed during the 1860s and 1870s by James Hinks of Birmingham, Great Britain, who successfully bred the bulldog with the now-extinct English white terrier. Bull terriers are strongly built, muscular, well-balanced and active dogs, with a keen, determined and intelligent expression. Their most recognizable features are their long oval-shaped head, slim bat-like ears and triangular-shaped eyes, which are small, dark and closely set. Their coats are flat, short and harsh to the touch with a fine gloss, and they range in colour from pure white or black, to brindle, red, fawn or tricolour.

Bull terriers walk with a jaunty gait and carry their tails horizontally, living up to their nickname of 'gladiator of the canine race'. Because of their power and temperament, they are not the ideal dog for the first-time owner, but if they are properly trained they make reliable pets. They don't always get on well with other dogs and are not completely trustworthy with other pets, especially cats. However, they are very affectionate creatures that love human company, they are particularly good with children, and they make formidable guard dogs.

Pet Profile

Despite the stigma attached to his breed, Henry is a very gentle white and red coloured bull terrier. He is not keen on sharing the house with Lucky the cat, however they keep their distance and are respectful of each other. He is a thinker and often has to stop to ponder what to do next at his own pace.

Here, Henry is in a bit of a dilemma. Should he play football or stop to gnaw on his biscuit bone? It's a dog's life, after all!

Henry

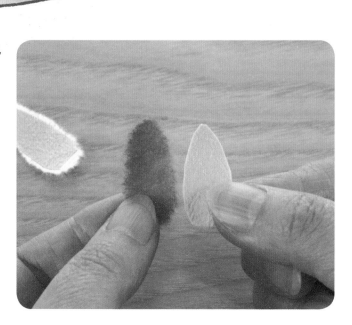

YOU WILL NEED:

- five A5 (21 x 15cm/8¼ x 5¾in) rectangles of handmade paper: one each in black, dark brown, pink, reddish-brown and white for the body, collar, ears, head, nose and tail
- two A5 (21 x 15cm/8¼ x 5¾in) rectangles of craft paper: one each in black and white for the ears and eyes
- one 3cm (1⅛in) length of 24-gauge white covered florists' wire for the tail
- one pink facial tissue
- teardrop punch
- gold coloured brass paper fastener
- basic tool kit (see pages 12–13)

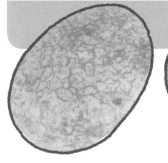

Pebble focus: for the body, you will need one broad bean-shaped pebble that is slightly plump at one end to suggest the rump. It should be about the same size as a hen's egg. For the head, you will need one oval- shaped pebble, approximately half of the size of the pebble used for the body.

1 To make the ears, use a pencil, ruler and scissors to mark, measure and cut out two 3 x 4cm (1⅛ x 1½in) rectangles for the inner ears: one each in pink handmade paper and white craft paper. For the outer ears, cut out two 2 x 3cm (¾ x 1⅛in) rectangles: one each in reddish-brown and white handmade paper. Following the instructions on page 20 and using the ear template below, make up the ears using pink handmade paper for the inner ear colouring. Be careful to make one ear's outer colouring reddish-brown and the other ear's outer colouring white. Set the ears aside.

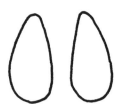

Bull terrier ear template

2 **To make the tail**, use a pencil and ruler to mark and measure out an isosceles triangle with a base of 2cm (¾in) and sides of 3cm (1⅛in) onto the white handmade paper. Tear it out and smear glue mix all over the paper. Place the florists' wire on top of the triangle's apex. Slant the paper at a slight angle and wind it spirally down, covering the wire by rotating it. Make sure that one end is pointed to create the tail's tip and the other end is slightly thicker to form the base of the tail. Set the tail aside.

3 Use the glue mix to cover both pebbles completely with pieces of white handmade paper. When the glue is dry, use a pencil to outline the place on the body pebble where the head pebble is to be attached.

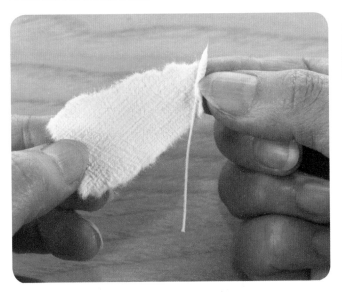

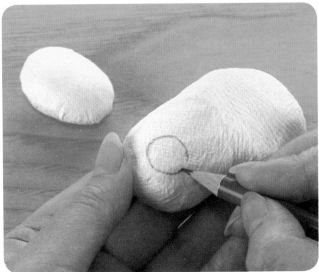

4 **To attach the patch and ears**, tear out a circular-shaped patch from reddish-brown handmade paper, the size of which should fill half of the forehead. Using the glue mix, attach this onto the appropriate part of the forehead. Attach the ears onto the back of the head using a little PVA adhesive. The pink inner ear should face towards the front of the dog. Use small pieces of reddish-brown and white handmade paper to hide the join between the ears and head.

5 Apply a little glue mix to the muzzle area and attach small pieces of pink facial tissue over the glued area. Tear out a thumb-tip sized circle from brown handmade paper. Apply a little glue mix to the paper and mould it into a triangular-shaped nose. Using a little PVA adhesive, attach it onto the tip of the muzzle. When the adhesive is dry, cover the nose with a layer of clear nail varnish.

6 **To make the eyes,** use a teardrop punch to create two teardrops from black craft paper. Using a drop of PVA adhesive, attach them onto the face in the desired position and add a tiny dot of white acrylic paint to each eye. When the paint is dry, cover the eyes with a layer of clear nail varnish. Use a grey brush-tip pen to draw on an upside down Y for the bull terrier's mouth.

7 **To make the body,** tear out one circular-shaped patch from reddish-brown handmade paper, the size of which should cover one side of the back. Tear out another patch, of a suitable size to cover the rump. Attach these patches onto their appropriate areas of the body using the glue mix.

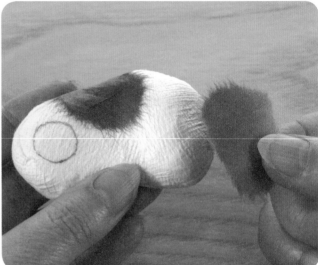

Take your time creating the facial details to get them just right for each breed. Bull terriers are known for their long, slim ears and slanted, closely set eyes, so take care when positioning these.

8 Using a little PVA adhesive, attach the base of the tail onto the underside of the body's back-end. Use a small piece of white handmade paper to hide the join between the tail and body.

9 **To join the pebbles**, use a pencil, ruler and scissors to mark, measure and cut out a 1 x 6cm (⅜ x 2⅜in) rectangle of white handmade paper. Following the instructions on page 18, join the head and body pebbles together, making sure that the paper ring is glued onto the outlined area created in step 3.

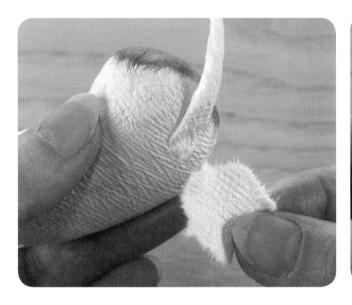

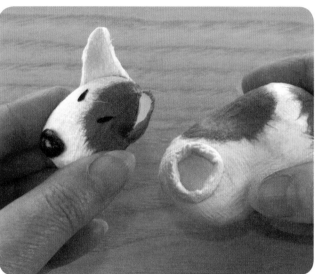

10 **Create the collar with a nametag** from black handmade paper and a gold coloured brass paper fastener, following the instructions on page 97. Fasten it around the dog's neck to hide the join between the two pebbles.

Henry's collar is functional as well as fashionable! In addition to giving him a smart appearance, it cleverly hides the joins between the head and body pebbles. See page 97 for making up instructions.

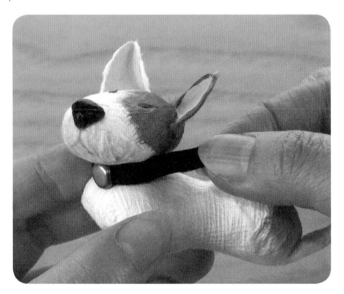

Dachshund

Toby

The dachshund is the short-legged, elongated dog breed belonging to the hound family. There are three sizes of the breed: standard, miniature and the lesser-known, rabbit-sized kaninchenteckel. Dachshunds exhibit three coat varieties: smooth hair, long hair and wire hair, and their colours and patterns vary, the dominant colours being red, or black and tan. The dachshund is known for its long face, flat medium-length rounded ears, elongated muscular body, short legs, and finely tapered tail carried in line with its back.

The temperament of dachshunds can vary greatly, but they are generally lively, intelligent and affectionate dogs that require an owner who understands their need for entertainment and exercise. They can often be strong-headed, stubborn and mischievous, making them a challenge to train, but they also display devotion to their owners and are loyal companions. Dachshunds only bark when necessary and have a particularly loud bark, making them good guard dogs despite their size.

Pet Profile

Toby is a very energetic, strong-willed miniature black and tan dachshund who is constantly on the go! Today he has been up to all sorts of mischief, chasing small animals and birds in the garden with great determination, then digging holes in the lawn and flowerbeds to bury any treasure he has found.

Toby is getting some well-earned rest on his cosy pink blanket, guarding his prized toy after the excitement of playing his favourite game of chase-me is over.

Toby

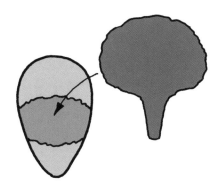

YOU WILL NEED:

- three A5 (21 x 15cm/8¼ x 5¾in) rectangles of handmade paper: one each in black, mustard yellow and reddish-brown for the body, ears, head and tail
- two A5 (21 x 15cm/8¼ x 5¾in) rectangles of craft paper: one each in red leather effect and white for the collar and ears
- one 3cm (1⅛in) length of 24-gauge white covered florists' wire for the tail
- basic tool kit (see pages 12–13)

Pebble focus: for the body, you will need one long jellybean-shaped pebble, about the same size as a hen's egg. For the head, you will need one egg-shaped pebble, approximately one-third of the size of the pebble used for the body.

1 **To make the ears**, use a pencil, ruler and scissors to mark, measure and cut out three 3 x 4cm (1⅛ x 1½in) rectangles: one each in black and mustard yellow handmade paper and white craft paper. Following the instructions on page 20 and using the ear template below, make up the ears using mustard yellow handmade paper for the inner ear colouring. Set the ears aside.

Dachshund ear template

2 **To make the tail**, use a pencil and ruler to mark and measure out an isosceles triangle with a base of 1cm (⅜in) and sides of 4cm (1½in) onto the black handmade paper. Tear it out and smear glue mix all over the paper. Place the florists' wire on top of the triangle's apex.

3 Slant the paper at a slight angle and wind it spirally down, covering the wire by rotating it. Make sure that one end is pointed to create the tail's tip and the other end is slightly thicker to form the base of the tail. Set the tail aside.

4 **To make the head**, use the glue mix to cover the smaller pebble completely with pieces of mustard yellow handmade paper.

5 Tear off a strip from brown handmade paper, the width of which should be approximately one-third of the head pebble's length and the length of which should be half the pebble's circumference. Using the glue mix, attach the strip horizontally across the middle of the pebble.

6 Tear out a mushroom-like shape from black handmade paper of a suitable size to cover between the nose (the pebble's pointed end) and the top of the head. Using the glue mix, attach it onto the appropriate part of the face.

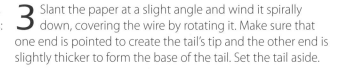

7 **Attach the ears** on top of the head using a little PVA adhesive. The mustard yellow inner ear should face towards the front of the dog and the ears should drape down. Use small pieces of black handmade paper to hide the join between the ears and head.

8 Tear out a fingertip-sized circle from black handmade paper. Apply a little glue mix to the paper and mould it into a triangular-shaped nose. Using a little PVA adhesive, attach it onto the tip of the face. When the adhesive is dry, cover the nose with a layer of clear nail varnish.

9 **To make the eyes**, once the PVA adhesive is dry, use a black brush-tip pen to draw two semicircular lines onto the dachshund's face to suggest closed eyes and an upside down Y for its mouth. Cut out two tiny circles from brown handmade paper and use a glue stick to attach them onto the face, slightly above the eyes.

10 **To make the body**, use the glue mix to cover the larger pebble completely with pieces of mustard yellow handmade paper. When the glue is dry, use a pencil to outline the area on the body pebble where the head pebble is to be attached.

11 Use the glue mix to cover the top of the body pebble with pieces of black handmade paper from the neck to the back-end. Using a little PVA adhesive, attach the base of the tail onto the body's back-end. Use a small piece of black handmade paper to hide the join between the tail and body.

12 **To join the pebbles**, use a pencil, ruler and scissors to mark, measure and cut out a 1 x 6cm (⅜ x 2⅜in) rectangle of black handmade paper. Following the instructions on page 18, join the head and body pebbles together, making sure that the paper ring is glued onto the outlined area created in step 10.

When attaching the pebbles together, angle the head pebble with the dog's nose pointing downwards to suggest a sleeping pose, which is enhanced by the drawn on closed eyelids.

13 **Create the collar with fastener** from red leather craft paper, following the instructions on page 97. Fasten it around the dog's neck to hide the join between the two pebbles.

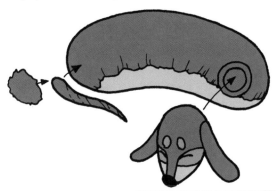

Jessie

Jessie is a very energetic beagle who loves nothing more than to relax on her favourite cushion after a long walk in the park. The beagle has been created using exactly the same techniques as for the dachshund. For the body, you will need a jellybean-shaped pebble and for the head, use an egg-like shaped pebble, approximately one-third of the size of the pebble used for the body.

Use pieces of white handmade paper to completely cover both pebbles and then add pieces of reddish-brown and black handmade papers on top to create tricolour fur. Attach a small piece of white handmade paper to the tail's tip. For the ears, use pieces of dark brown handmade paper for the outer ear, light brown handmade paper for the inner ear and white craft paper. Jessie's plain dog collar is created from brown handmade paper following the instructions on page 96. To create the bone, bowl and cushion see pages 99–100.

Labradors

Benjamin & Coca

The Labrador is one of several kinds of retriever, a type of gun dog thought to be the most popular breed worldwide. They are also the most well-known breed of assistance dogs, being widely used as a police dogs, rescue dogs and guide dogs due to their detection and working abilities. Labradors are relatively large dogs that are characterized by their short smooth coats and straight, powerful tails. They exhibit three recognized coat colours: solid black; yellow, ranging from light cream or gold to 'fox-red'; and chocolate brown.

Labradors are extremely lovable and attentive dogs, lively, carefree and playful in attitude. Their friendly and affectionate temperaments make them good with children, visitors and other family pets. Although they can be somewhat boisterous if untrained, Labradors respond very well to praise and positive attention. They are prone to chewing objects but can be trained out of this type of behaviour, and they usually hold objects in their mouths with great gentleness.

Pet Profile

Benjamin, a cream-coloured Labrador, and Coca, his chocolate-coloured friend are six month old puppies who love nothing better than playing together. Very soon, they will have their first taste of guide dog training, as their owner will be introducing them to the sights, sounds and smells of a world in which they will play such an important part.

Benjamin and Coca are 'food and fun' orientated dogs that love to play a game of tag with their favourite toy before going home for a tasty snack.

Benjamin

YOU WILL NEED:

- five A5 (21 x 15cm/8¼ x 5¾in) rectangles of handmade paper: one each in dark blue, dark brown, cream, pink and yellow for the body, collar, ears, head, tail and toy ring
- two A5 (21 x 15cm/8¼ x 5¾in) rectangles of craft paper: one each in black and white for the ears and eyes
- two 3cm (1⅛in) lengths of 24-gauge white covered florists' wire: one each for the tail and toy ring
- flower petal punch
- green coloured brass paper fastener
- basic tool kit (see pages 12–13)

Pebble focus: for the body, you will need one pear-shaped pebble about the same size as a hen's egg. For the head, use one oval-shaped pebble, approximately half of the size of the pebble used for the body.

1 To make the ears, use a pencil, ruler and scissors to mark, measure and cut out three 2.5 x 3cm (1 x 1⅛in) rectangles: one each in light cream and pink handmade paper and white craft paper. Following the instructions on page 20 and using the ear template below, make up the ears using pink handmade paper for the inner and outer ear colouring. Set the ears aside.

Labrador ear template

2 To make the tail, wrap small amounts of cotton wool around a length of florists' wire, making a long French bean-like shape approximately 0.5cm (³⁄₁₆in) in diameter. Using a pencil and ruler, mark and measure out a 1.5 x 3cm (⅝ x 1⅛in) rectangle onto the cream handmade paper. Tear it out and smear glue mix all over the paper.

3 Place the wire and cotton wool on top of the paper's right-hand side. Slant the paper at a slight angle and wind it spirally down, covering the wire by rotating it. Make sure that one end is pointed to create the tail's tip and the other is slightly thicker to form the base of the tail. Set the tail aside.

4 To make the head, use the glue mix to cover the smaller pebble completely with pieces of cream handmade paper.

5 Attach the ears onto the back of the head using a little PVA adhesive. The pink inner ear should face towards the front of the dog. Use small pieces of cream handmade paper to hide the join between the ears and head.

6 When the PVA adhesive is dry, fold the ears up at their base. Fold the tip of each ear down at the halfway point, so that they hang close to the head.

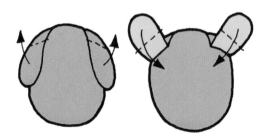

7 Tear out a fingertip-sized circle from dark brown handmade paper. Apply a little glue mix to the paper and mould it into a triangular-shaped nose. Using a little PVA adhesive, attach the nose onto the tip of the face.

8 Use a grey brush-tip pen to draw a stretched out W for the Labrador's mouth. Draw small ovals at either end of the W, to make the location points for attaching on the toy ring.

9 **For the toy ring**, wrap small amounts of cotton wool around the remaining length of florists' wire to thicken it out a little. Use a pencil, ruler and scissors to mark, measure and cut out a 1.5 x 4cm (⅝ x 1½in) rectangle of yellow handmade paper. Smear glue mix all over the paper.

10 Place the wire and cotton wool on top of the paper's right-hand side. Slant the paper at a slight angle and wind it spirally down, covering the wire by rotating it. Continue to the end of the wire.

11 When the glue is dry, cleanly cut a tiny piece from each end of the paper and wire and discard them. Gently curve the paper covered wire into a three-quarters ring-like shape. Using a little PVA adhesive, attach its ends onto the W's ovals that were drawn on in step 8.

12 **To make the eyes**, use a flower petal punch to create two petals from black craft paper. Using a drop of PVA adhesive, attach them onto the face in the desired position and add a tiny dot of white acrylic paint to each eye. When the paint is dry, cover the eyes and nose with a layer of clear nail varnish.

13 **To make the body**, use the glue mix to cover the larger pebble completely with pieces of cream handmade paper. When the glue is dry, use a pencil to outline the area on the body pebble where the head pebble is to be attached.

14 Cleanly cut a tiny piece from the base of the tail and discard it. Using a little PVA adhesive, attach the tail via its base onto the top of the body's back-end. When the adhesive is dry, gently curve the tail to suggest a happy wagging tail.

15 **To join the pebbles**, use a pencil, ruler and scissors to mark, measure and cut out a 1 x 6cm (⅜ x 2⅜in) rectangle of light cream handmade paper. Following the instructions on page 18, join the head and body pebbles together, making sure that the paper ring is glued onto the outlined area created in step 13.

16 **Create the collar with nametag** from dark blue handmade paper and a green coloured brass paper fastener, following the instructions on page 97. Fasten it around the dog's neck to hide the join between the two pebbles.

When attaching the head to the body pebble, angle the head slightly upwards. This will create a playful pose, giving the impression that Benjamin is offering his toy ring to his owner to throw for him.

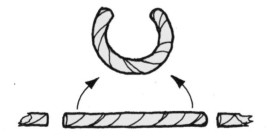

Coca

This quiet and contented Labrador is created using the same sized pebble and exactly the same techniques as for Benjamin (see pages 72–73). Simply change the colour of the handmade papers to a darker brown to match his coat colouring. For this variation, use a grey brush-tip pen to draw on a wide smile instead of adding the toy ring. Coca's collar with nametag is made following the instructions on page 97 using dark pink handmade paper and a white coloured brass paper fastener.

Dottie

The Dalmatian is a popular breed of dog, noted for its white coat with either black or liver spots. Dottie is a very active dog that needs plenty of exercise and she craves human companionship. She is created using similar sized pebbles and the same techniques as for the Labrador (see pages 72–73).

Use white handmade paper to completely cover the pebbles. Punch spots of various dimensions from black craft paper and glue them all over the body. Make the tail slightly longer than the Labrador's and use a grey brush-tip pen to add an elongated W shape for her smile. Dottie's collar with nametag is created following the instructions on page 97, using red handmade paper and a yellow coloured brass paper fastener.

Schnauzer

Ash

Schnauzers originated in Germany and were descended from herding, ratting and guardian breeds of the Middle Ages. The name comes from the winning show dog at the 3rd International Show held in Hanover in 1879. In German 'schnauz bart' means 'conspicuous moustache or beard' and schnauzers are known for the long hair spouting from around their noses. Their coats are typically stiff, wiry and salt-and-pepper or black in colour. This hair is non-shedding and will grow much like human hair, therefore it needs to be regularly cut and groomed.

The schnauzer is a robust and sturdy working dog, known for being intelligent and easy to train. They have a regal and aristocratic appearance and are quite versatile to keep as family pets. Their inquisitive and energetic temperaments require a strong willed owner who can be constant and firm with training and commands. The schnauzer thrives on human companionship and does not do well if left alone for extended periods of time. They are very protective of their family and are generally aloof and reserved with strangers, making eager guard dogs in the home.

Pet Profile

Ash is constantly exploring, learning and testing his limits. He is highly energetic and looks forward to his long, daily walk. He loves spending time with his owner, especially when he is being groomed to keep his soft and dense undercoat free of tangles and in top condition.

Ash is constantly alert and on guard even when relaxing at home after an energetic game of 'fetch'. Here, he is standing over his bowl to protect his food from potential intruders.

Ash

YOU WILL NEED:

- five A5 (21 x 15cm/8¼ x 5¾in) rectangles of handmade paper: one each in black, blue-grey, brown, dark grey and white for the body, collar, ears, head, nose and tail
- two A5 (21 x 15cm/8¼ x 5¾in) rectangles of craft paper: one each in black and white for the ears and eyes
- circle punch
- basic tool kit (see pages 12–13)

Pebble focus: for the body, you will need one slightly rounded rectangular-shaped pebble about the size of a hen's egg. For the head, use one egg-like shaped pebble, approximately half the size of the pebble used for the body.

1 To make the ears, use a pencil, ruler and scissors to mark, measure and cut out three 2 x 3cm (¾ x 1⅛in) rectangles: two from blue-grey handmade paper and one from white craft paper. Following the instructions on page 20 and using the ear template below, make up the ears using blue-grey handmade paper for the inner and outer ear colouring. Set the ears aside.

3 To make the head, use the glue mix to cover the smaller pebble completely with pieces of white handmade paper. Treating the pebble's pointed end as the top of the head, cover two-thirds of it (from the pointed end down) with pieces of blue-grey handmade paper. Be careful to leave the white paper area of the remaining third clear (the large rounded end), as later on this will become the muzzle.

4 Attach the ears onto the back of the head using a little PVA adhesive. The blue-grey inner ear should face towards the front of the dog. When the adhesive is dry, fold the ears down at their halfway point, so that they hang close to the head. Use small pieces of blue-grey handmade paper to hide the join between the ears and head.

Schnauzer ear template

2 To make the tail, tear out a fingertip-sized circle from dark grey handmade paper. Apply a little glue mix to the paper and mould it into a tail. The tail should be approximately the same size as an oat grain.

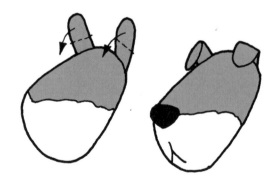

5 Use a grey brush-tip pen to draw on an upside down Y for the schnauzer's mouth onto the muzzle.

6 Tear out a fingertip-sized circle from black handmade paper. Apply a little glue mix to the paper and mould it into a triangular-shaped nose. Use a little PVA adhesive to attach the nose onto the tip of the muzzle.

7 **To make the eyes**, use a circle punch to create two circles from black craft paper. Using a drop of PVA adhesive, attach them onto the face so that they are positioned in the middle, between the ears and nose.

8 Tear out a circle from white handmade paper, approximately the same size as a garden pea. Cut the circle in half.

9 Use a drop of PVA adhesive, attach the semicircles onto the head with their straight edges pointing downwards. Position each semicircle above each eye to suggest the eyebrows. Add a tiny dot of white acrylic paint to each eye. When the paint is dry, cover the eyes and nose with a layer of clear nail varnish.

The schnauzer's bushy eyebrows are created by attaching semicircles of white handmade paper above each eye. Along with his small beady eyes and folded ears, they help to give Ash an alert and intelligent expression.

10 **To make the body**, use the glue mix to cover the larger pebble completely with pieces of white handmade paper. When the glue is dry, use a pencil to outline the areas where the tail and the head pebbles are to be attached.

11 Using the glue mix, attach pieces of grey handmade paper onto the top and on either side of the body, being careful to leave the white paper areas of the chest and underside clear.

12 Cleanly cut a tiny piece from the end of the tail to create a straight edge. Discard the cut off piece. Using a little PVA adhesive, attach the straight edge of the tail onto the outlined area created in step 10.

13 **To join the pebbles**, use a pencil, ruler and scissors to mark, measure and cut out a 1 x 6cm (⅜ x 2⅜in) rectangle of brown handmade paper. Following the instructions on page 18, join the head and body pebbles together, making sure that the paper ring is glued onto the outlined area created in step 10.

14 **Make the plain collar** from brown handmade paper, following the instructions on page 96. Fasten it around the dog's neck to hide the join between the two pebbles.

Angus

The Scottish terrier, also known as the Scottie or Aberdeen terrier, is a breed of dog best known for its distinctive profile, black colour and typical terrier personality. This handsome dog, Angus, can be created using similar shaped pebbles and techniques as for the schnauzer.

Use black handmade paper to cover both pebbles and all other body parts. The tail and ears are made using the same techniques as for the Westie on pages 82–83. Angus' plain collar is simply created following the instructions on page 96 and using bright yellow handmade paper.

Westie

Baz

West Highland white terriers, commonly know as Westies, are descended from Cairn terriers and Scottish terriers, which often produced white puppies. They are commonly bred for hunting and are well known for their distinctive white coats, which consist of a soft, dense undercoat and rough outer coat that requires regular grooming. The general appearance of the Westie is that of a small, well-balanced, proud and strong terrier, deep in the chest and back ribs with a straight back and muscular hindquarters. However, much of the dog's charm comes from its small, erect ears, which are set wide apart and come to a distinctive point.

West Highland white terriers make intelligent, curious and friendly dogs, that are fairly easy to train. They are alert and eager to please in temperament and are noted for their retentive memory. The Westie makes an excellent family pet and does equally well in the city as in a more rural environment – as long as the dog receives the amount of attention from its owner that it feels it deserves. Whether it lives in an apartment or a large house, the Westie is always ready to retrieve a ball, chew a bone, or curl up on its owner's lap.

Pet Profile

Baz is a very friendly and sociable dog, although he has a tendency for getting into mischief when he is left alone in the backyard; he has been known to bark loudly at his neighbours and steal food from the cat's bowl. He loves to be admired and wears his blue diamanté collar with pride.

Baz thoroughly enjoys daydreaming about catching pigeons at the local park whilst sitting on his homemade purple cushion (see making up instructions on page 99).

Baz

YOU WILL NEED:

- two A5 (21 x 15cm/8¼ x 5¾in) rectangles of handmade paper: one each in blue and white for the body, collar, ears, head, nose and tail
- two A5 (21 x 15cm/8¼ x 5¾in) rectangles of craft paper: one each in black and white for the ears and eyes
- one 2cm (¾in) length of 24-gauge white covered florists' wire for the tail
- one pink facial tissue
- flower petal punch
- strip of tiny sticky-backed gems
- basic tool kit (see pages 12–13)

Pebble focus: for the body, you will need one teardrop-shaped pebble with a slightly flat base, so it will sit up without wobbling. It should be about the same size as a hen's egg. For the head, use one round pebble, approximately half the size of the pebble used for the body.

1 To make the ears, use a pencil, ruler and scissors to mark, measure and cut out three 2 x 3cm (¾ x 1⅛in) rectangles: two from white handmade paper and one from white craft paper. Following the instructions on page 20 and using the ear template below, make up the ears using white handmade paper for the inner and outer ear colouring. Set the ears aside.

Westie ear template

2 To make the tail, use a pencil and ruler to mark and measure out an isosceles triangle with a base of 2cm (¾in) and sides of 3cm (1⅛in) onto the white handmade paper. Tear it out and smear glue mix all over the paper. Place the florists' wire on top of the triangle's apex.

3 Slant the paper at a slight angle and wind it spirally down, covering the wire by rotating it. Make sure that one end is pointed to create the tail's tip and the other end is slightly thicker to form the base of the tail. Set the tail aside.

4 To make the head, add a small amount of modelling clay to the surface of the smaller pebble. Using a modelling spatula, mould the clay into a slightly raised bun-shaped muzzle. Let the clay dry. Using the glue mix, cover the pebble and clay completely with pieces of white handmade paper.

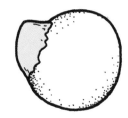

5 Attach the ears on top of the head using a little PVA adhesive. The white inner ear should face towards the front of the dog. Use small pieces of white handmade paper to hide the join between the ears and head. Add an extra piece of white handmade paper to each cheek to suggest a layer of long fur.

Make sure that you attach the ears so that they are positioned slightly apart and erect – the Westie is known for its small, pointed ears.

6 Tear out a fingertip-sized circle from black handmade paper. Apply a little glue mix to the paper and mould it into a triangular-shaped nose. Using a little PVA adhesive, attach the nose onto the tip of the muzzle. When the adhesive is dry, use a grey brush-tip pen to draw on an upside down Y for the Westie's mouth.

7 **To make the eyes**, use a flower petal punch to create two petals from black craft paper. Using a drop of PVA adhesive, attach them onto the face positioning them just above the nose and add a tiny dot of white acrylic paint to each eye. When the paint is dry, cover the eyes and nose with a layer of clear nail varnish.

8 **To make the body**, use the glue mix to cover the larger pebble completely with pieces of white handmade paper.

9 Tear out a circular piece from white handmade paper. This should be approximately the same size as the smaller pebble. Using the glue mix, attach the paper onto the top of the body to suggest a layer of long fur. Roll the glued area between the palms of your hands to smooth the paper down.

10 When the glue is dry, use a pencil to outline the area on the body pebble where the head pebble is to be attached.

11 Using a little PVA adhesive, attach the base of the tail onto the underside of the body's back-end. Use a small piece of white handmade paper to hide the join between the tail and body.

12 **To join the pebbles**, use a pencil, ruler and scissors to mark, measure and cut out a 1 x 6cm (⅜ x 2⅜in) rectangle of white handmade paper. Following the instructions on page 18, join the head and body pebbles together, making sure that the paper ring is glued onto the outlined area created in step 10. Try to position the head pebble so that it is looking upwards slightly.

13 **Make the collar with fastener** from blue handmade paper, following the instructions on page 97. Fasten it around the dog's neck to hide the join between the two pebbles. Decorate the surface with tiny sticky-backed gems to create a diamanté collar.

By positioning the head slightly upwards, Baz is able to show off his sparkling collar with pride.

Boston Terrier

Chappy

The Boston terrier is America's first native purebred, developed in 1891 in Boston, Massachusetts by crossing the English bulldog with the now extinct English white terrier. The Boston terrier is a typically small, compactly built breed with a short tail and a square-shaped muzzle, which should be free of wrinkles. They have erect ears which are located at the corners of the skull and large, round eyes that are set wide apart, giving them an alert but gentle expression. Their coats are characteristically marked with white in proportion to black, brindle, seal or a combination of the three.

Boston terriers generally have friendly, very strong and playful personalities and they love to be around people, although their temperaments can range from those that are eager to please their master to those that are more stubborn. Both types can be easily trained, given a patient and assertive owner. Boston terriers are well behaved around children, elderly people and strangers, and they generally get on well with other pets. If you can provide the right environment for a Boston, it will become an affectionate, lifelong friend.

Pet Profile

Chappy is a very intelligent, eager-to-please Boston terrier, whose appealing round eyes will melt your heart. He is relatively inactive indoors and is quite content to spend time at home with his elderly owners. He has a habit of sleeping on his master's favourite armchair, but is not easily offended if anyone expresses a desire to sit beside him.

The Boston terrier has been nicknamed the 'American Gentleman' because of its dapper appearance. Chappy's owner has made him a smart red bowtie, which he is very happy to wear (see page 98).

Chappy

YOU WILL NEED:

- four A5 (21 x 15cm/8¼ x 5¾in) rectangles of handmade paper: one each in black, dark brown, red and white for the body, bowtie, ears, head and tail
- two A5 (21 x 15cm/8¼ x 5¾in) rectangles of craft paper: one each in black and white for the ears and eyes
- one 2cm (¾in) length of 24-gauge white covered florists' wire for the tail
- circle punch
- basic tool kit (see pages 12–1

Pebble focus: for the body, you will need one leaning teardrop-shaped pebble with a slightly flat base so that it will sit up without wobbling. It should be about the same size as a hen's egg. For the head, use one round pebble, approximately half the size of the pebble used for the body.

1 **To make the ears**, use a pencil, ruler and scissors to mark, measure and cut out three 3 x 4cm (1⅛ x 1½in) rectangles: one each in black and dark brown handmade paper and white craft paper. Following the instructions on page 20 and using the ear template below, make up the ears using dark brown handmade paper for the inner ear colouring. Set the ears aside.

3 Slant the paper at a slight angle and wind it spirally down, covering the wire by rotating it. Continue to the end of the wire. When the glue is dry, twist the paper-covered wire into a tight curl to create the Boston terrier's crinkly tail. Set the tail aside.

Boston terrier ear template

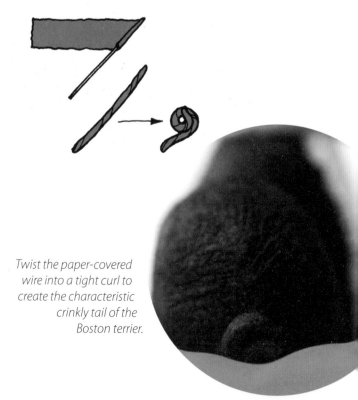

2 **To make the tail**, use a pencil, ruler and scissors to mark, measure and cut out a 0.5 x 2.5cm (³⁄₁₆ x 1in) rectangle of black handmade paper. Smear glue mix all over the paper. Place the florists' wire on top of the right-hand side of the paper.

Twist the paper-covered wire into a tight curl to create the characteristic crinkly tail of the Boston terrier.

4 **To make the head**, add a small amount of modelling clay to the surface of the smaller pebble. Using a modelling spatula, mould the clay into a squashed bun-shaped muzzle with an upside down V indentation, as shown below. Let the clay dry. Using the glue mix, cover the pebble and clay completely with pieces of white handmade paper.

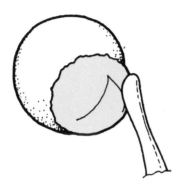

5 When the glue is almost dry, use a vellum embossing tool to carefully press the paper into the upside down V indentation.

6 Using the glue mix, cover the cheeks, the area of the eyes and back of the head with pieces of black handmade paper, being careful to leave the white paper areas of the muzzle and forehead clear.

7 **Attach the ears** onto the back of the head using a little PVA adhesive. The dark brown inner ear should face towards the front of the dog and the ears should be erect. Use small pieces of black handmade paper to hide the join between the ears and head.

8 Tear out a fingertip-sized circle from black handmade paper. Apply a little glue mix to the paper and mould it into a triangular-shaped nose. Using a little PVA adhesive, attach the nose above the indentation's tip.

9 Use a grey brush-tip pen to draw an upside down V inside the indentation made in step 5 to suggest the Boston terrier's mouth. Lightly shade in the area between the nose and the top part of the lips.

10 **To make the eyes**, use a circle punch to create two circles from black craft paper. Using a glue stick, attach them onto a piece of white craft paper. Echoing the eye shape, trim the craft paper leaving a border of approximately 1mm (1⁄16in) around each circle. Using a drop of PVA adhesive, attach them onto the face at a similar height to the nose, setting them wide apart.

11 Add a tiny dot of white acrylic paint to each eye. When the paint is dry, cover the eyes and nose with a layer of clear nail varnish.

12 **To make the body**, use the glue mix to cover the larger pebble completely with pieces of black handmade paper and the chest area with pieces of white handmade paper. When the glue is dry, use a pencil to outline the area on the body pebble where the head pebble is to be attached.

13 Using a little PVA adhesive, attach the tail on to the underside of the body's back-end. Use a small piece of black handmade paper to hide the join between the tail and body.

14 **To join the pebbles**, use a pencil, ruler and scissors to mark, measure and cut out a 1 x 6cm (3⁄8 x 2 3⁄8in) rectangle of black handmade paper. Following the instructions on page 18, join the head and body pebbles together, making sure that the paper ring is glued onto the outlined area created in step 12. Try to position the head pebble so that it is looking upwards and leaning to one side slightly.

15 **Create the bowtie** from red handmade paper, following the instructions on page 98. Fasten it around the dog's neck to hide the join between the two pebbles.

Shiba Inu

Kai

The Shiba Inu is the smallest of all the indigenous Japanese breeds. They have existed in the Sanin region of Japan for centuries and were originally bred for hunting. *Inu* is the Japanese word for dog and *Shiba* can mean either a type of red shrub or something tiny, which perfectly describes the colour and build of the breed. The Shiba Inu has a double coat, consisting of a straight outer coat and a soft, dense undercoat. Its coats is usually a shade of red, sesame or black and tan, and white. They are seasonally heavy shedders, producing a relatively large amount of fur in proportion to their size. They are recognized for their pointed muzzles, dark noses, small eyes, broad foreheads and triangular pricked-up ears. They also carry a spitz-like tail that is thick, strong and curls over their backs.

A very bold, lively and sweet breed; the Shiba Inu makes a good companion and gets on very well with children. They are intelligent, alert and wary of strangers, making them good guard dogs. They seldom bark, preferring to shriek in an extraordinary manner. This energetic, loyal and docile dog is both active and rapid, and, like all spitz-type dogs, it is extremely clean.

Pet Profile

Kai is a clean and fastidious dog who will go out of his way to keep his coat immaculate, doing all he can to avoid stepping in puddles, mud and dirt. When sufficiently provoked or unhappy, Kai will produce a loud, high-pitched scream. He has also been known to emit a similar sound when very happy or excited, for example when his owner picks up his lead for walkies.

Kai is very happy relaxing indoors on his favourite soft cushion which he enjoys sitting up on to groom his glossy coat. Instructions for the cushion are given on page 125.

Kai

YOU WILL NEED:

- six A5 (21 x 15cm/8¼ x 5¾in) rectangles of handmade paper: one each in black, dark pink, orange, reddish-brown, white and wine for the body, collar, ears, head and tail
- two A5 (21 x 15cm/8¼ x 5¾in) rectangles of craft paper: one each in black and white for the ears and eyes
- one 4cm (1½in) length of 24-gauge white covered florists' wire for the tail
- teardrop punch
- wine coloured brass paper fastener
- basic tool kit (see pages 12–13)

Pebble focus: for the body, you will need one broad bean-shaped pebble that is slightly plump at one end to suggest the rump. It should be about the same size as a hen's egg. For the head, use one round pebble, approximately half the size of the pebble used for the body.

1 To make the ears, use a pencil, ruler and scissors to mark, measure and cut out three 2 x 3cm (¾ x 1⅛in) rectangles: one each in dark pink and reddish-brown handmade paper and white craft paper. Following the instructions on page 20 and using the ear template below, make up the ears using dark pink handmade paper for the inner ear colouring. Set the ears aside.

Shiba Inu ear template

2 To make the tail, wrap small amounts of cotton wool around the florists' wire, making a long French bean-like shape, approximately 5mm (³⁄₁₆in) in diameter.

3 Tear out a paddle-like shape from white handmade paper, 2 x 5cm (¾ x 2in) in size. Smear glue mix all over the paper. Wrap the paper around the wire and cotton wool so that its sides overlap a little and shape one end slightly into a point to create the tail's tip.

4 Tear out a paddle-like shape from orange handmade paper, 0.8 x 5cm (⁵⁄₁₆ x 2in) in size. Attach it onto the tail using the glue mix, working from the tip to base and being careful to cover up the overlap. Set the tail aside.

5 To make the head, add a small amount of modelling clay to the surface of the smaller pebble. Using a modelling spatula, mould the clay into a paper cup-shaped muzzle. Let the clay dry. Using the glue mix, cover the pebble and clay with pieces of white handmade paper.

The Shiba Inu's tail is thick and bushy and is characteristically carried in a curl over its back.

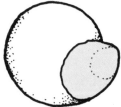

6 Using the glue mix, cover the face with pieces of orange handmade paper, starting from the muzzle's tip and finishing at the top of the head. Then add pieces of reddish-brown handmade paper from the forehead to the back of the head to suggest the fur's gradational colouring.

7 **Attach the ears** onto the back of the head using a little PVA adhesive. The dark pink inner ear should face towards the front of the dog. Use small pieces of reddish-brown handmade paper to hide the join between the ears and head.

8 Tear out a fingertip-sized circle from black handmade paper. Apply a little glue mix to the paper and mould it into a triangular-shaped nose. Using a little PVA adhesive, attach the nose onto the tip of the muzzle. When the adhesive is dry, use a grey brush-tip pen to draw a stretched out W for the mouth.

9 **To make the eyes,** use the small teardrop punch to create two teardrops from black craft paper. Using a drop of PVA adhesive, attach them onto the face in the desired position and add a tiny dot of white acrylic paint to each eye. When the paint is dry, cover the eyes and nose with a layer of clear nail varnish.

10 **To make the body,** use the glue mix to cover the larger pebble completely with pieces of white handmade paper. When the glue is dry, use a pencil to lightly mark the line of the spine, working from the neck to the back-end. Outline the area where the head pebble is to be attached.

11 Use the glue mix to attach pieces of orange handmade paper to most of the body, being careful to leave the white paper areas of the chest and underside clear. From reddish-brown handmade paper, tear out a strip measuring 1cm (⅜in) in width and the same length as the body. Use a glue stick to attach the strip along the line of the spine to create the fur's gradational colouring along the back.

12 Using a little PVA adhesive, attach the base of the tail onto the underside of the body's back-end. Use a small piece of white handmade paper to hide the join between the tail and the body. When the adhesive is dry, twist the tail into a curl, which is carried over the dog's back.

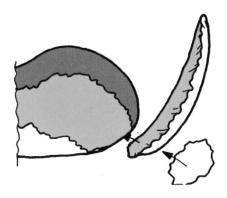

13 **To join the pebbles,** use a pencil, ruler and scissors to mark, measure and cut out a 1 x 6cm (⅜ x 2⅜in) rectangle of reddish-brown handmade paper. Following the instructions on page 18, join the head and body pebbles together, making sure that the paper ring is glued onto the outlined area created in step 10.

14 **Create the collar with nametag** from wine handmade paper and a wine coloured brass paper fastener, following the instructions on page 97. Fasten it around the dog's neck to hide the join between the two pebbles.

Hana

Akitas make excellent pets as they are loyal and docile in temperament and are generally clean and quiet. The Akita is created using exactly the same techniques as the Shiba Inu. For the body and head, you will need pebbles of a similar shape that are slightly larger than those used for the Shiba Inu and which suggest a 'sitting up' pose in their shape.

Use white handmade paper for the Akita's main coat colouring and reddish-brown handmade paper for the ears and other markings. Hana's hanging diamanté dog collar is made following the instructions on page 96, using red handmade paper and sticky-backed gems.

Cocker Spaniel

Oscar

The English cocker spaniel is a breed of gun dog. Cocker spaniels are sturdy, compact and well-balanced working dogs. They have dark eyes and long ears that reach to their noses when pulled forward, which gives them an alert and intelligent expression. A cocker spaniel's nose can be black or brown depending on its coat colour. Their coats are of medium length and come in either solid black, liver or red, or part-colour combinations of white with black, liver or red markings.

Due to its happy disposition and continuously wagging tail, the cocker spaniel has been nicknamed 'The Merry Cocker'. They are a sensitive breed of dog, and when handled with tenderness and respect they make willing learners. Cocker spaniels make joyful, entertaining and active pets; they are excellent with children; and they get along very well with other dogs and family pets. They are sociable with strangers and respectfully obey any commands they are given. Cocker spaniels have a typical lifespan of 11–12 years.

Pet Profile

As with most cocker spaniels, Oscar is happy having a brisk walk every morning and evening and looks forward to a long country walk at the weekend. If allowed off the lead, he loves to run through the undergrowth, explore muddy places and get himself very wet while swimming in the river.

Oscar enjoys going out into the garden during the day and will spend many happy hours bouncing around after his favourite tennis ball (see making up instructions on page 101).

Oscar

YOU WILL NEED:

- two A5 (21 x 15cm/8¼ x 5¾in) rectangles of sandy-brown coloured handmade paper for the body, ears, head and tail
- four A5 (21 x 15cm/8¼ x 5¾in) rectangles of handmade paper: one each in brown, dark brown, pink and yellow for the collar, ears, nose, tennis ball and tongue
- two A5 (21 x 15cm/8¼ x 5¾in) rectangles of craft paper: one each in black and white for the ears and eyes
- one 8cm (3⅛in) length of 24-gauge white covered florists' wire for the tail
- flower petal punch
- basic tool kit (see pages 12–13)

Pebble focus: for the body, you will need one bean-shaped pebble that has a slight curve to one side, about the same size as a hen's egg. For the head, use one egg-shaped pebble, approximately one-third of the size of the pebble used for the body.

1 **To make the ears,** use a pencil, ruler and scissors to mark, measure and cut out three 4cm (1½in) squares: one each in pink and sandy-brown handmade paper and white craft paper. Following the instructions on page 20 and using the ear template below, make up the ears using pink handmade paper for the inner ear colouring. Set the ears aside.

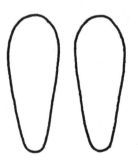

Cocker spaniel ear template

2 **To make the tail,** tear out a fingertip-sized circle from sandy-brown handmade paper. Apply a little glue mix to the paper and mould it into a tail. The tail should be approximately the same size as an oat grain.

3 **To make the head,** use the glue mix to cover the smaller pebble completely with pieces of sandy-brown handmade paper.

4 **Attach the ears** on top of the head by their narrow end, using a little PVA adhesive. The pink inner ear should face towards the side of the dog and they should drape down. Use small pieces of sandy-brown handmade paper to hide the join between the ears and head.

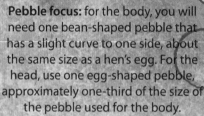

5 Tear out a fingertip-sized circle from dark brown handmade paper. Apply a little glue mix to the paper and mould it into a triangular-shaped nose. Using a little PVA adhesive, attach the nose onto the tip of the face. When the adhesive is dry, use a grey brush-tip pen to draw a stretched out W for the spaniel's mouth.

6 Cut out a tongue shape from pink handmade paper, approximately the same size as an oat grain. Use a drop of PVA adhesive to attach it via one end onto the line of the mouth so that it protrudes out.

With his long floppy ears and pink tongue poking out from his cheeky smile, Oscar is simply irresistible!

7 **To make the eyes**, use a flower punch to create two petals from black craft paper. Using a drop of PVA adhesive, attach them onto the face in the desired position and add a tiny dot of white acrylic paint to each eye. When the paint is dry, cover the eyes, nose and tongue with a layer of clear nail varnish.

8 **To make the body**, use the glue mix to cover the larger pebble completely with pieces of sandy-brown handmade paper. When the glue is dry, use a pencil to outline the area where the head pebble is to be attached.

9 Cleanly cut a tiny piece from the end of the tail to create a straight edge and discard the cut off piece. Using a little PVA adhesive, attach the tail via its straight edge onto the top of the body's back-end. Try to position the tail so that it leans to one side slightly and points in the same direction as the head to suggest a playful pose.

10 **To join the pebbles**, use a pencil, ruler and scissors to mark, measure and cut out a 1 x 6cm (⅜ x 2⅜in) rectangle of sandy-brown handmade paper. Following the instructions on page 18, join the head and body pebbles together, making sure that the paper ring is glued onto the outlined area created in step 8. Try to position the head pebble so that it is looking upwards slightly.

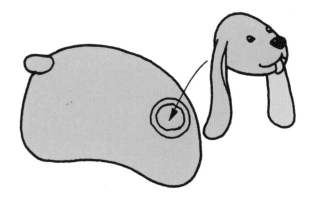

11 **Create the plain collar** from dark brown handmade paper, following the instructions on page 96. Fasten it around the dog's neck to hide the join between the two pebbles.

The spaniel's bright-eyed expression is achieved by adding a tiny dot of white acrylic paint to each eye and covering with a layer of clear nail varnish.

Accessories

Over the next few pages, you will discover a wonderful range of cute and colourful accessories to treat your canine friends. Choose from a fabulous collection of collars to embellish your pooch, from plain to diamanté, or even a smart bowtie! Give your dog some creature comforts with a cosy blanket or cushion to relax on and create a range of tasty treats including a food bowl and succulent bone. You will even find a range of toys for your dog to play with, including a tennis ball and ball and rope toy.

Plain Collar

An understated yet stylish collar that can be made up in a variety of colours.

1 Using a pencil, ruler and scissors, mark, measure and cut out a 1.5 x 7cm (⅝ x 2¾in) rectangle of coloured handmade paper. Place the rectangle sideways on and divide it into three across its width by first folding the bottom edge up and then folding the top edge down. Attach the layers of paper together using a little PVA adhesive.

2 Place the collar around the dog's neck, so that its ends overlap slightly. Attach the ends together using a little PVA adhesive.

Hanging Diamanté Collar

The perfect collar for smart dogs that like a little more sparkle.

1 Repeat steps 1 and 2 of the plain collar. Using a pencil, ruler and scissors, mark, measure and cut out a 0.3 x 1.5cm (⅛ x ⅝in) rectangle of handmade paper in the same colour as the collar. Turn the rectangle lengthways on and decorate it with tiny sticky-backed gems.

2 Attach the back of the decorated rectangle via one end onto the front of the collar using a drop of PVA adhesive.

  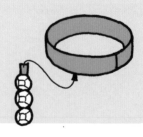

Collar with Fastener

A simple-to-make collar that can be decorated with sticky-backed gems for a diamanté effect if desired.

1 Repeat step 1 of the plain collar on page 96 using coloured handmade paper. Cut off the top and bottom left-hand corners from the collar to make a point.

2 To make the fastener, use a pencil, ruler and scissors to mark, measure and cut out a 0.3 x 1cm (⅛ x ⅜in) rectangle of handmade paper in the same colour as the collar.

3 Place the collar around the dog's neck, so that its ends overlap slightly and place the fastener vertically on top of them. Use a little PVA adhesive to attach the fastener's top and bottom edges down at the back of the collar.

4 For a diamanté effect, decorate the surface of the collar with tiny sticky-backed gems.

Collar with Nametag

Your dog will never go astray – with this collar he will wear his name with pride.

1 Open out a brass paper fastener by pulling its prongs apart. Press down on the fastener's middle section to flatten the prongs out to either side. Turn the fastener over.

2 Use a pencil, ruler and scissors to mark, measure and cut out two 1.5 x 3cm (⅝ x 1⅛in) rectangles of coloured handmade paper. Turn the rectangles and fastener sideways on.

3 From either side of the fastener, slide the paper rectangles underneath the prongs, being careful that they go between the prongs and the fastener's middle section, as shown. Using a drop of PVA adhesive, attach each prong centrally onto the adjacent paper rectangle.

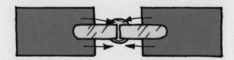

4 Divide each rectangle into three across its width by first folding the bottom edge up and then the top edge down. Attach the layers of paper together using a little PVA adhesive.

5 When the adhesive is dry, carefully curve the brass fastener's prongs into a ring-like shape. Place the collar around the dog's neck, so that its ends overlap slightly. Attach the ends together using a little PVA adhesive.

Bowtie

The smartest accessory for top dogs.

1 Repeat steps 1 and 2 of the plain dog collar on page 96 using coloured handmade paper.

2 Use a pencil, ruler and scissors to mark, measure and cut out a 2 x 2.5cm (¾ x 1in) rectangle of handmade paper in the same colour as the collar. Place the rectangle sideways on and fold it in half from top to bottom. Attach the layers of paper together using a little PVA adhesive.

3 Pleat and gather the middle of the paper to form a bow.

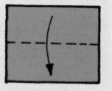
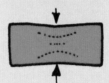

4 **To make the bow's centre band**, use a pencil, ruler and scissors to mark, measure and cut out a 0.3 x 1cm (⅛ x ⅜in) rectangle of handmade paper in the same colour as the collar. Place the band vertically over the middle of the bow. Use a little PVA adhesive to attach the band's top and bottom edges at the back of the bow and fasten them onto the collar.

Blanket

Your dog will love to lay his head down on this cosy blanket decorated with paw prints.

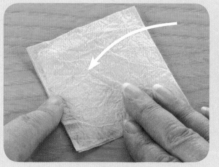

1 Use a pencil, ruler and scissors to mark, measure and cut out a 8 x 16cm (3⅛ x 6¼in) rectangle of coloured handmade paper. Make a thin cushion of cotton wool, approximately 7cm (2¾in) square in size. Place the cushion onto the centre of the left-hand section of the paper and run a line of PVA adhesive around its edges.

2 Carefully fold the paper in half from right to left and press the edges neatly together.

3 Use a brown felt-tip pen to draw around the edges of the blanket. Decorate the top surface of the blanket using a paw-print pen.

Cushion

The perfect resting spot for your pooch.

1 Use a pencil, ruler and scissors to mark, measure and cut out the illustrated cushion template below onto coloured handmade paper. Make sure that the three joining tabs are no less than 0.5cm (³⁄₁₆in) wide. Insert fold-lines in place as shown.

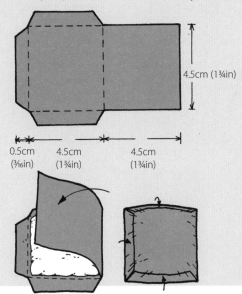

4.5cm (1¾in)

0.5cm (³⁄₁₆in)   4.5cm (1¾in)   4.5cm (1¾in)

2 Shape cotton wool into a square, approximately 4.5cm (1¾in) square and 1cm (³⁄₈in) thick in size. Place the cotton wool padding onto the centre of the left-hand section of the paper. Fold the right-hand side over to the left along the existing fold-line, taking care not to press the cushion flat. Apply a little PVA adhesive onto each of the tabs.

3 Fold the tabs over along their existing fold-lines and onto the cushion's top surface. Press them down gently.

Food Bowl

An essential accessory for that all-important dinner time.

1 Hand-roll a small amount of modelling clay to a thickness of approximately 2mm (⅛in). Use a ruler, compasses and modelling spatula to measure, mark and cut out a rectangle, measuring 1 x 8cm (⅜ x 3⅛in) and a circle of clay measuring 2.5cm (1in) in diameter.

2 Wrap the rectangle around the circumference of the circle, making sure to press their edges firmly together. Let the clay dry. Use the glue mix to cover the food bowl completely with pieces of coloured handmade paper.

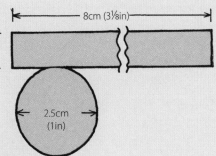

8cm (3⅛in)

1cm (³⁄₈in)

2.5cm (1in)

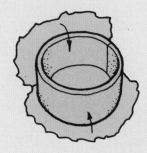

Water Bowl

Essential for a refreshing drink after a long walk in the park.

1 Hand-roll a small amount of modelling clay to a thickness of approximately 2mm (⅛in). Use a ruler, compasses and modelling spatula to measure, mark and cut out a 1 x 6 x 8cm (⅜ x 2⅜ x 3⅛in) arch-like shape and a 2.5cm (1in) diameter circle of clay.

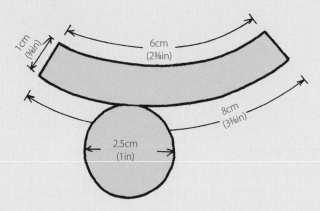

2 Wrap the arch by its longer edge around the circumference of the circle, making sure to press their edges firmly together. Let the clay dry. Use the glue mix to cover the water bowl completely with pieces of coloured handmade paper.

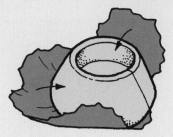

Bone

Your dog will be your best friend when you give him this tasty treat.

1 Mould a piece of modelling clay into a bone-like shape measuring approximately 3.5cm (1⅜in) in length and 5mm (³⁄₁₆in) in thickness. Let the clay dry.

2 Use the glue mix to cover the bone completely with pieces of white handmade paper.

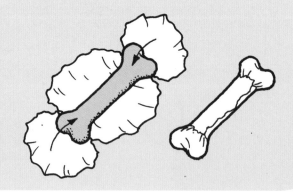

Ball with Rope

The perfect toy to take to the park or garden.

1 Hand-roll a clay ball to a diameter of 1cm (⅜in). Using a modelling spatula, make a hole into the ball's surface. Let the clay dry.

2 Use the glue mix to cover the ball completely with pieces of coloured handmade paper.

3 Cut a 6cm (2⅜in) length of coloured cord and loop it in half. Poke the ends of the cord through the paper and into the ball's hole. Secure them in place with a drop of PVA adhesive.

Tennis Ball

Your dog will tire himself out chasing after this brightly coloured ball.

1 Hand-roll a clay ball to a diameter of 1cm (⅜in). Let the clay dry. Use the glue mix to cover the ball completely with pieces of yellow handmade paper.

2 When the glue is dry, use white acrylic paint and a fine paint-brush to paint swirly stitch markings onto the tennis ball.

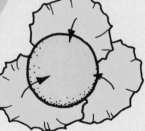

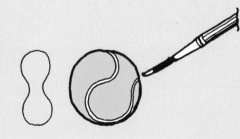

COVETED CATS

Playful, serene, enigmatic and adorable, cats have always inspired pleasure. From the svelte and muscular Japanese bobtail to the elegant Siamese, the timid and reserved Russian blue to the everyday moggy, a beautiful variety of cats are all waiting in this section to be created by your nimble fingers. Each of the pebble cats has been given its own whimsical personality captured with simple facial details, guaranteed to bring a smile to your face.

A number of typical cat poses have been captured here for you to re-create, including the sitting up pose of the tortoiseshell moggies, the grooming stance adopted by the Siamese, and the comfortable curled up and napping positions of the ginger and bobtail cats. Don't be limited by the breeds we have chosen – each of these poses can be adapted for any breed and coat colour of your choice. By altering the proportions of

the head and body pebbles together with your choice of colours and textures of handmade paper, you are able to create almost any breed of cat or kitten.

Having mastered the techniques in the previous sections, you should now be able to create the projects that follow with very little difficulty. You may wish to start with the Napping Ginger chapter (see page 104–109), which provides full step-by-step instructions to guide you through how to join your pebbles to create a realistic feline pose, before moving on to re-create the other cat breeds featured. You will be spoilt for choice with the vast array of accessories to be made following the instructions on pages 122–125, including a wide range of collars, a tasty fishbone treat and a cosy cushion perfect for cat naps. Use our instructions as a guide and let your imagination run wild, but most of all, have fun with your felines.

Napping Ginger

Lady

Cats are the world's best sleepers, slumbering away approximately 60 per cent of their lives. They conserve energy by sleeping more than most animals, especially as they grow older. As a cat is so efficient at obtaining its protein-rich food, it has plenty of time to rest up for its next hunting trip – or visit to the kitchen! A typical feline day includes over 15 hours of sleeping and dozing and 4 to 6 hours of grooming and playing, with hunting, eating and exploring making up the rest of the time. Some cats can sleep as much as 20 hours in a 24 hour period.

The colour ginger is nature's natural antidepressant. It promotes a joyful atmosphere even in the gloomiest of places. Ginger cats have even purred their way into the hearts of great leaders. Sir Winston Churchill, the politician and wartime Prime Minister who led Britain to victory in World War II, owned several ginger cats in his lifetime. Apparently, his favourite ginger tabby, Jock, slept in his bed every night and was taken to all the wartime Cabinet meetings.

Pet Profile

Lady is a keen hunter and expresses a lot of interest in the small creatures that visit the garden. When indoors, Lady is a very happy, contented and laid-back cat, spending most of her time having a well-deserved nap on her favourite cushion or sitting on the window shelf watching the world go by.

Cats are never happier than when they are spending a lazy afternoon sleeping in the warmth and comfort of a loving home. To make this cosy cushion, see page 125.

Lady

YOU WILL NEED:

- four A5 (21 x 15cm/8¼ x 5¾in) rectangles of handmade paper: one each in dark pink, ginger striped (if unobtainable use ginger), pink and white for the body, collar, ears, head and tail
- one A5 (21 x 15cm/8¼ x 5¾in) rectangle of white craft paper for the ears
- one 7cm (2¾in) length of 24-gauge white covered florists' wire for the tail
- one pink facial tissue
- basic tool kit (see pages 12–13)

Pebble focus: for the body, you will need one round kidney bean-shaped pebble, about the same size as a hen's egg. For the head, use one fairly flat circular-shaped pebble, approximately one-third of the size of the pebble used for the body.

1 **To make the ears**, use a pencil, ruler and scissors to mark, measure and cut out three 2 x 3cm (¾ x 1⅛in) rectangles: one each in pink and ginger striped handmade paper and white craft paper. Following the instructions on page 20 and using the ear template below, make up the ears using pink handmade paper for the inner ear. Set the ears aside.

Napping ginger ear template

2 Use the glue mix to cover both pebbles completely with pieces of white handmade paper. When the glue is dry on the larger pebble, use a pencil to lightly mark the line of the spine, working from the top of the neck to the back-end. Also outline the area where the smaller pebble is to be attached.

3 **To make the face**, tear out three fingertip-sized circles from white handmade paper and apply a little glue mix to each circle. Roll two of the circles into tight balls measuring approximately 3mm (⅛in) in diameter. Mould the remaining circle into a long shape, similar in size to a grain of rice.

4 Divide the grain's length approximately into quarters. Cut off one quarter for the cat's chin and use the remaining three-quarters for the nose. Arrange the two balls, chin and nose into the configuration as shown.

5 Use a little PVA adhesive to attach the two balls side by side onto the smaller pebble's outside edge to suggest the lips. Attach the nose vertically above and the chin vertically below, being careful to place them adjacent to the lips to make the muzzle.

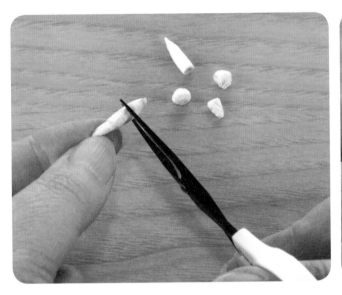

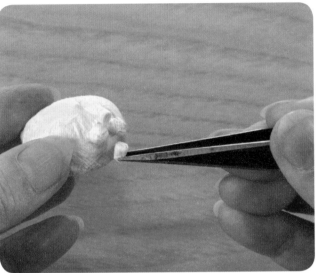

6 Using the glue mix, attach small pieces of white handmade paper over the muzzle then layer small pieces of pink facial tissue on top. When the glue is almost dry, use a vellum embossing tool to carefully apply pressure to the area of paper between the chin, lips and nose to make an X-like indentation.

7 **To attach the ears**, use the glue mix to cover the eye and forehead areas with pieces of ginger striped handmade paper. Attach the ears onto the back of the head using a little PVA adhesive, with the pink inner ear facing towards the front of the cat. Use small pieces of ginger striped handmade paper to hide the join between the ears and head.

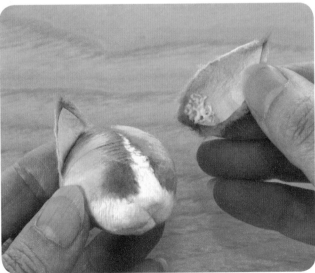

8 **For the whiskers**, follow the instructions on page 23 using beading thread or clear nylon fishing line. Attach the whiskers in place on either side of the cat's nose using a drop of PVA adhesive. When the adhesive is dry, use a grey brush-tip pen to draw two semicircular lines onto the cat's face to suggest closed eyes (see page 22).

9 **To make the tail**, wrap small amounts of cotton wool around the florists' wire making a long French bean-like shape approximately 5mm (³⁄₁₆in) in diameter. Tear out a paddle-like shape from ginger striped handmade paper 2 x 7cm (¾ x 2¾in) in size. Smear glue mix all over the paper. Wrap the paper around the wire and cotton wool, so that its sides overlap a little and shape one end slightly into a point to create the tail's tip. Set the tail aside.

Draw on semicircles using grey brush-tip pen to create the peaceful sleeping expression. If you would prefer your cat to be wide awake, follow the instructions for making open wide and bright eyes on page 22.

10 **To make the body**, tear out an oval from ginger striped handmade paper of a suitable size to cover the length and half the circumference of the larger pebble. Use the glue mix to attach the oval onto the body along the line of the spine. Using a little PVA adhesive, attach the base of the tail onto the body's back-end. Use a small piece of ginger striped handmade paper to hide the join between the tail and body. When the adhesive is dry, gently curve the tail along the side of the body so that it points towards the head.

11 **To join the pebbles**, use a pencil, ruler and scissors to mark, measure and cut out a 1 x 6cm (⅜ x 2⅜in) rectangle of ginger striped handmade paper. Following the instructions on page 18, join the head and body pebbles together, making sure that the paper ring is glued onto the outlined area created in step 2.

12 **Create the ribbon collar** from dark pink handmade paper, following the instructions on page 123. Place the ends of the collar around the cat's neck, and tie a reef (square) knot at the back to hide the join between the two pebbles.

Sasha

The Russian blue is an intelligent cat renowned for its gentleness and affectionate nature. Sasha is slightly overweight and very spoiled by her owner. She is made using the same techniques as for the ginger cat to create the same sleeping pose.

For the head and body pebbles, you will need pebbles shaped like slightly squashed buns. The body pebble should be about the same size as a hen's egg and should sit comfortably in the palm of your hand. The head pebble should be approximately one-third of the size of the body pebble. Use blue-brown handmade paper for the coat's colouring. Sasha's hanging diamanté cat collar is made using dark blue handmade paper and sticky-backed gems, following the instructions on page 122.

Grooming Siamese

The Siamese is one of the first distinctly recognized breeds of Oriental cat. The exact origin of the breed is unknown, but they are believed to originate from southeast Asia, descended from the sacred temple cats of Siam (now Thailand). Siamese cats are well known for their creamy base coats with coloured points on their muzzles, ears, paws and lower legs and long tapering tails. Their eyes are typically bright blue and almond-shaped. Siamese cats are long-lived, with an average life-span of 15 to 20 years.

Siamese cats can be extremely vocal, with a loud, low-pitched voice – known as 'meezer', from which the Siamese gets its nickname. Siamese are affectionate and intelligent cats, renowned for their social nature. They display a great need for human friendship and will often bond strongly with their owner. However, the Siamese still needs the companionship of other pets and will get along with almost any type of gentle animal, including other cats and dogs. When the cat gets together with another of its own species it then becomes a great source of fun and enjoyment!

Tai Tai

Pet Profile

No cat has more to say than Tai Tai. If you do not talk to her, she will challenge you to do so! Tai Tai is quintessentially a people's cat that loves to be in your lap, asleep on the duvet, or playing games with a ball of scrunched-up paper.

Tai Tai is busy grooming her coat after eating a tasty piece of her favourite fish. To make up the plate and fishbone, see page 124.

Tai Tai

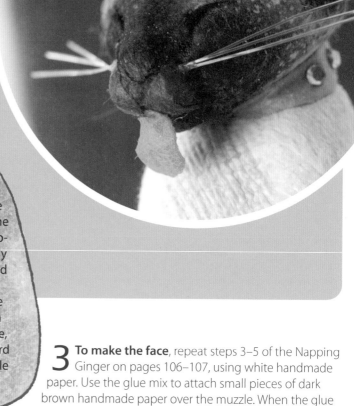

YOU WILL NEED:

- three A5 (21 x 15cm/8¼ x 5¾in) rectangles of handmade paper: one each in dark brown, dark pink and white for the body, collar, ears, head, tail and tongue
- one A5 (21 x 15cm/8¼ x 5¾in) rectangle of white craft paper for the ears
- one 7cm (2¾in) length of 24-gauge white covered florists' wire for the tail
- strip of tiny sticky-backed gems
- basic tool kit (see pages 12–13)

Pebble focus: for the body, you will need one tall triangular teardrop-shaped pebble, slightly twisted to one side and about the same size as a hen's egg. For the head, use one flattish circular-shaped pebble, approximately one-third of the size of the pebble used for the body.

1 **To make the ears**, use a pencil, ruler and scissors to mark, measure and cut out three 2 x 3cm (¾ x 1⅛in) rectangles: one each in dark brown and dark pink handmade paper and white craft paper. Following the instructions on page 20 and using the ear template below, make up the ears using dark pink handmade paper for the inner ear colouring. Set the ears aside.

Grooming Siamese ear template

2 Use the glue mix to cover both pebbles completely with pieces of white handmade paper. When the glue is dry, use a pencil to outline the area on the larger pebble where the smaller pebble is to be attached. Position it slightly to one side of the pebble's top point.

3 **To make the face**, repeat steps 3–5 of the Napping Ginger on pages 106–107, using white handmade paper. Use the glue mix to attach small pieces of dark brown handmade paper over the muzzle. When the glue is almost dry, use a vellum embossing tool to carefully apply pressure to the area of paper between the chin, lips and nose to make an X-like indentation.

4 **Attach the ears** onto the back of the head using a little PVA adhesive, with their pink inner ear facing towards the front of the cat.

5 **For the whiskers**, follow the instructions on page 23 using beading thread or clear nylon fishing line. Attach the whiskers in place on either side of the cat's nose using a drop of PVA adhesive. When the adhesive is dry, use a black brush-tip pen to draw two semicircular lines onto the cat's face to suggest closed eyes.

6 **For the licking tongue**, cut out a tongue shape from pink handmade paper, approximately the same size as an oat grain. Use a drop of PVA adhesive to attach it via one end between the cat's lips and chin.

It is important to include the dark pink tongue to give Tai Tai her characteristic grooming pose. Tai Tai's face needs to be slightly angled to groom those hard-to-reach places.

7 **To make the tail**, wrap small amounts of cotton wool around the florists' wire, making a long thin French bean-like shape, approximately 3mm (⅛in) in diameter. Tear out a paddle-like shape from dark brown handmade paper, 1.5 x 7cm (⅝ x 2¾in) in size. Smear glue mix all over the paper.

8 Wrap the paper around the wire and cotton wool, so that its sides overlap a little and shape one end slightly into a point to create the tip of the Siamese's long, thin tail.

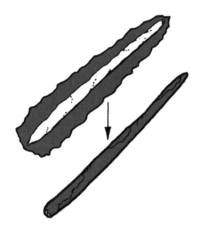

9 **To make the body**, use the glue mix to attach pieces of dark brown handmade paper around the base of the body pebble to suggest the coloured areas on the Siamese's front and back paws. Using a little PVA adhesive, attach the base of the tail onto the underside of the body's back-end. Use a small piece of dark brown handmade paper to hide the join between the tail and body. When the adhesive is dry, gently curve the tail along the side of the body so that it points towards the front (see illustration for step 10).

10 **To join the pebbles**, use a pencil, ruler and scissors to mark, measure and cut out a 1 x 6cm (⅜ x 2⅜in) rectangle of white handmade paper. Following the instructions on page 18, join the head and body pebbles together, making sure that the paper ring is glued onto the outlined area created in step 2. Try to position the head pebble to look downwards slightly to suggest a grooming pose.

11 **Create the plain collar** from dark pink handmade paper, following the instructions on page 122. Fasten it around the cat's neck to hide the join between the two pebbles. Decorate its surface with tiny sticky-backed gems to create a diamanté collar.

Lucky

Lucky is a tabby, one of the most popular breeds of cat. She is similar in pose to the Siamese and uses the same techniques for her assembly.

For the head and body, you will need slightly plump teardrop-shaped pebbles. The body pebble should be about the same size as a hen's egg and should sit comfortably in the palm of your hand. The pebble used for the head is approximately one-third the size of the pebble used for the body. Use brown striped, patterned handmade paper for Lucky's coat colouring. Her plain collar is made from dark pink handmade paper, following the instructions on page 122.

Curled Up Bobtail

Spot

The Japanese bobtail is a breed of cat with an unusual short 'bobbed' tail more closely resembling the tail of a rabbit than that of an ordinary feline. These small domestic cats originated in Japan and southeast Asia and can now be found throughout the world. Japanese bobtails are characteristically svelte and muscular, with a rounded muzzle and a triangular head. They have oval-shaped eyes and large, broad ears that are set well apart. The cat's coat is soft and silky and can be found in a number of colours. The most commonly seen coat pattern is the tricolour, consisting of white, red and black fur. Japanese bobtails are extremely friendly and intelligent cats. Their soft voices can make a scale of tones and some people say they sing. They adore human companionship and almost always speak when spoken to, sometimes carrying on 'conversations' with their owners. They are easy to teach tricks, such as walking on a harness and lead, and playing fetch. They have a sweet nature and get on well with most other animals and children, and so they make good family pets.

Pet Profile

Spot is an affectionate and generally sweet-tempered Japanese bobtail, who enjoys spending time with her owners when she is not asleep. Although Spot likes to talk, she is never overly noisy but has a soft tone to her 'meow'. She is a strong and active cat that appreciates exercise and enjoys a good game of chase-the-string.

After playing with a ball of wool, Spot has tired herself out and is now curled up completely in a deep sleep, twitching her whiskers as she dreams.

Spot

YOU WILL NEED:

- four A5 (21 x 15cm/8¼ x 5¾in) rectangles of handmade paper: one each in black, dark brown, red and white for the body, collar, ears, head and tail
- two A5 (21 x 15cm/8¼ x 5¾in) rectangles of craft paper: one each in black and white for the ears and dot on the nose
- one 2cm (¾in) length of 24-gauge white covered florists' wire for the tail
- one pink facial tissue
- small circle punch
- basic tool kit (see pages 12–13)

Pebble focus: for the body, you will need one round bean-shaped pebble, about the same size as a hen's egg. For the head, use a fairly flat circular-shaped pebble, approximately one-third of the size of the pebble used for the body.

1 **To make the ears**, use a pencil, ruler and scissors to mark, measure and cut out three 2 x 3cm (¾ x 1⅛in) rectangles: one each in black and dark brown handmade paper and white craft paper. Following the instructions on page 20 and using the ear template below, make up the ears using dark brown handmade paper for the inner ear colouring. Set the ears aside.

3 **To make the face**, repeat steps 3–6 of the Napping Ginger on pages 106–107, using white handmade paper, pink facial tissue and a vellum embossing tool. Use a circle punch to create a circle from black craft paper. Attach the circle onto the face just to one side of the nose using a drop of PVA adhesive.

Curled up bobtail ear template

Spot gets her name from the black mark found on one side of her nose. By angling her head to one side and drawing on semi-circles for her closed eyes, she adopts a very relaxed pose.

2 Use the glue mix to cover both pebbles completely with pieces of white handmade paper. When the glue is dry, use a pencil to outline the area on the larger pebble where the smaller pebble is to be attached. Try to position it slightly near the larger pebble's base and smaller end. Lightly mark the line of the spine along the pebble's outside edge, working from the neck to the back-end.

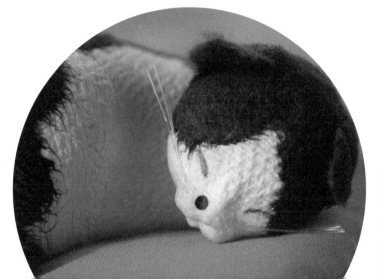

4 **To attach the ears**, use the glue mix to cover the forehead and back of the head with pieces of black handmade paper. Attach the ears onto the back of the head using a little PVA adhesive, with the dark brown inner ear facing towards the front of the cat. Use small pieces of black handmade paper to hide the join between the ears and head.

5 **For the whiskers**, follow the instructions on page 23 using beading thread or clear nylon fishing line. Attach the whiskers in place on either side of the cat's nose and flat towards the face, using a drop of PVA adhesive. When the adhesive is dry, use a grey brush-tip pen to draw two semicircular lines onto the cat's face to suggest closed eyes.

6 **To make the tail**, wrap small amounts of cotton wool around one end of the florists' wire, to make a cotton-bud shape, approximately 1cm (⅜in) in length. Tear out a piece of black handmade paper that is slightly larger than the bud and smear glue mix all over the paper. Wrap the paper around the bud so that its sides overlap a little, being careful to maintain the bud's shape. Set the tail aside.

7 **To make the body**, use the glue mix to attach pieces of black handmade paper along the line of the spine, large rump area and back-end. Using a little PVA adhesive, attach the base of the tail via its wired end onto the body's back-end. Use a small piece of black handmade paper to hide the join between the tail and body. When the adhesive is dry, gently press the tail flat against the body so that it points towards the head.

The Japanese bobtail is characterized by its short tail, which wraps around the body in a distinctive curve.

8 **To join the pebbles**, use a pencil, ruler and scissors to mark, measure and cut out a 1 x 6cm (⅜ x 2⅜in) rectangle of white handmade paper. Following the instructions on page 18, join the head and body pebbles together, making sure that the paper ring is glued onto the outlined area created in step 2. Try to position the head pebble to look towards the tail, resting against the ground.

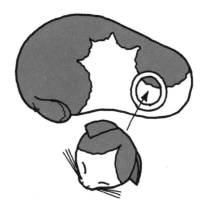

9 **Create the ribbon collar** from red handmade paper, following the instructions on page 123. Place the ends of the collar around the cat's neck, and tie a reef (square) knot at the back to hide the join between the two pebbles.

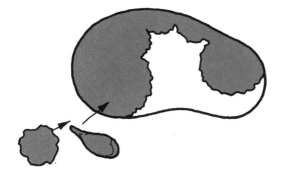

Izumo

This adorable, fawn-coloured Japanese bobtail kitten is created using exactly the same techniques as the black and white bobtail, adopting the same curled up pose. For the head and body, you will need similar shaped pebbles to those used for Spot, but they need to be slightly smaller in size. For the head, use a pebble approximately half the size of the pebble used for the body.

Cover both pebbles with white handmade paper then add fawn-coloured handmade paper to most parts of the body, ears, head and tail. Izumo's diamanté collar is made from blue handmade paper and embellished with sticky-backed gems, following the instructions on page 122.

Sitting Tortoiseshells

Maddie & Mimmi

'Moggy' is an affectionate term for a domestic cat, but is also used as an alternative name for a mongrel or mixed-breed cat whose ancestry and pedigree are unknown or only partially known. There are over six hundred million pet cats in homes all over the world. Of these, the vast majority are non-pedigree or crossbred cats; their parentage may be unknown, or neither of the parents a registered pedigree. However, as every proud owner knows, a healthy, happy moggy in the prime of its life can be every bit as magnificent in appearance and manner as a pedigree. The term 'tortoiseshell' or 'torties' for short is usually reserved for cats with brindled coats that have relatively little or no white markings. A tortoiseshell coat is characteristically mottled, with patches of red and black, chocolate, or cinnamon. The sizes of the cat's patches can vary from a speckled pattern to large areas of colour. The markings on a tortoiseshell cat are usually asymmetrical. The tortoiseshell is not a specific breed of cat and the tortoiseshell markings appear in many different cat breeds.

Pet Profile

Maddie and her kitten Mimmi are tortoiseshell moggies who love to play together before grooming one another's coats. Their 'belly-up' sitting position is a very vulnerable posture as it indicates total trust of each other.

Maddie and her kitten Mimmi spend most of their waking hours interacting with one another. Mimmi loves to play with the bell that adorns her mother's collar (see page 123 for making up instructions).

Maddie

YOU WILL NEED:

- six A5 (21 x 15cm/8¼ x 5¾in) rectangles of handmade paper: one each in black, dark brown, lavender, orange, pink and white for the body, collar, ears, head and tail
- two A5 (21 x 15cm/8¼ x 5¾in) rectangles of craft paper: one each in black and white for the ears and eyes
- one 6cm (2⅜in) length of 24-gauge white covered florists' wire for the tail
- one pink facial tissue
- teardrop punch
- small brass bell
- basic tool kit (see pages 12–13)

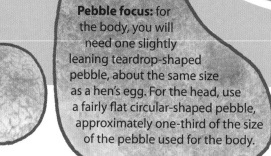

Pebble focus: for the body, you will need one slightly leaning teardrop-shaped pebble, about the same size as a hen's egg. For the head, use a fairly flat circular-shaped pebble, approximately one-third of the size of the pebble used for the body.

1 **To make the ears**, use a pencil, ruler and scissors to mark, measure and cut out three 2 x 3cm (¾ x 1⅛in) rectangles: one each in black and pink handmade paper and white craft paper. Following the instructions on page 20 and using the ear template below, make up the ears using pink handmade paper for the inner ear colouring. Set the ears aside.

Sitting tortoiseshell ear template

2 Use the glue mix to cover both pebbles completely with pieces of white handmade paper. When the glue is dry, use a pencil to outline the area on the larger pebble where the smaller pebble is to be attached. Try to position it at the top end of the pebble.

3 **To make the face**, repeat steps 3–6 of the Napping Ginger on pages 106–107, using white handmade paper, pink facial tissue and a vellum embossing tool.

4 Use the glue mix to cover the forehead and back of the head with small pieces of black, dark brown and orange handmade paper to suggest tortoiseshell markings.

Maddie's face is mottled, with asymmetrical patches of black, dark brown and orange, characteristic of tortoiseshells.

5 **Attach the ears** onto the back of the head using a little PVA adhesive, with their pink inner ear facing towards the front of the cat. Use small pieces of the appropriately coloured handmade paper to hide the join between the ears and head.

6 **For the whiskers**, follow the instructions on page 23 using beading thread or clear nylon fishing line. Attach the whiskers in place on either side of the cat's nose using a drop of PVA adhesive. Use a teardrop punch to create two teardrops from black craft paper. Attach them onto the face using a drop of PVA adhesive.

7 **To make the tail**, wrap small amounts of cotton wool around the florists' wire to make a long French bean-like shape, approximately 5mm (³⁄₁₆in) in diameter. Tear out a paddle-like shape from black handmade paper, 2 x 6cm (¾ x 2⅜in) in size. Smear glue mix all over the paper. Wrap the paper around the wire and cotton wool, so that its sides overlap a little and shape one end slightly into a point to create the tail's tip.

8 Tear out a fingertip-sized patch from orange handmade paper. Using the glue mix, attach it onto the tail as desired. Set the tail aside.

9 **To make the body**, use the glue mix to attach pieces of black, dark brown and orange handmade paper randomly onto the body pebble to suggest tortoiseshell markings. Using a little PVA adhesive, attach the base of the tail onto the underside of the body's back-end. Use a small piece of the appropriately coloured handmade paper to hide the join between the tail and body. When the adhesive is dry, gently curve the tail alongside of the body so that it points towards the front.

10 **To join the pebbles**, use a pencil, ruler and scissors to mark, measure and cut out a 1 x 6cm (⅜ x 2⅜in) rectangle of white handmade paper. Following the instructions on page 18, join the head and body pebbles together, making sure that the paper ring is glued onto the outlined area created in step 2. Try to position the head pebble to look downwards slightly.

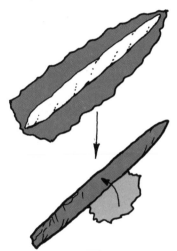

11 **Create the collar with bell** from lavender handmade paper and a brass bell, following the instructions on page 123. Fasten it around the cat's neck to hide the join between the two pebbles.

Mimmi

This enchanting kitten is created using exactly the same techniques as the sitting tortoiseshell. For the body and head, you will need pebbles that are slightly rounder and about half the size of the adult cat. To make up the ears, use the template provided below.

The tail has been made a little shorter and the head has been glued onto the body so that it is angled upwards, looking towards its mother.

Sitting tortoiseshell kitten ear template

Accessories

What better way is there to pamper your feline friend than with this irresistible range of miniature accessories? Find a wide selection of pretty yet practical collars that will make your cat look gorgeous whilst at the same time hiding the join between the head and body pebbles. Make a comfortable cushion for those cats that like nothing better than to curl up in a ball and sleep by the fire all day and for a tasty treat, create a fishbone for your cat to enjoy. Each accessory is so simply to make, you can pamper your pet by making up the whole range!

Plain Collar

Make this up in a flash using a colour of your choice.

1 Use a pencil, ruler and scissors to mark, measure and cut out a 1.2 x 6cm (½ x 2⅜in) rectangle of coloured handmade paper. Place the rectangle sideways on and divide it into three across its width by first folding the bottom edge up and then folding the top edge down. Attach the layers of paper together using a little PVA adhesive.

2 Place the collar around the cat's neck, so that its ends overlap slightly. Attach the ends together using a little PVA adhesive.

3 For a diamanté effect, decorate the surface of the collar with tiny sticky-backed gems.

Hanging Diamanté Collar

Perfect for fancy felines that just love a little sparkle!

1 Repeat steps 1 and 2 of the plain collar. Use a pencil, ruler and scissors to mark, measure and cut out a 0.3 x 1.5cm (⅛ x ⅝in) rectangle of the handmade paper in the same colour as the collar.

2 Turn the rectangle lengthways on and decorate it with tiny sticky-backed gems. Attach the back of the decorated rectangle via one end onto the front of the collar using a drop of PVA adhesive.

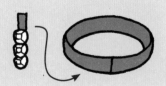

Collar with a Bell

Hear your cat coming with this cute collar embellished with a tiny brass bell.

1 Repeat steps 1 and 2 of the plain collar using coloured handmade paper.

2 Attach a small brass bell onto a length of double thread and tighten the thread against the bell with a knot. Attach the thread to the front of the collar, using a little PVA adhesive at the back. Trim off any excess thread.

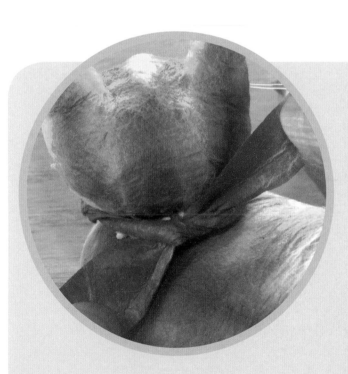

Ribbon Collar

The ribbon tie adds elegance and beauty to this collar.

1 Use a pencil, ruler and scissors to mark, measure and cut out a 0.8 x 12cm (⁵⁄₁₆ x 4¾in) rectangle of coloured handmade paper.

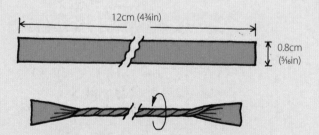

12cm (4¾in)

0.8cm (⁵⁄₁₆in)

2 Twist the paper's middle section so that it becomes string-like, forming the ribbon collar. Place the ends of the collar around the cat's neck, and tie a reef (square) knot at the back.

Plate

Your cat will need this plate to hold their tasty treats. See below for how to make up the fishbone.

1 Hand-roll a small amount of modelling clay to a thickness of approximately 2mm (¹⁄₁₆in). Use a ruler, compasses and a modelling spatula to measure, mark and cut out a 4cm (1½in) diameter circle of clay. Onto the circle, lightly mark a 2.5cm (1in) diameter inner circle, as shown.

2 Hand-roll a thin sausage of modelling clay long enough to fit around the circumference of the inner circle. Attach both parts together, as shown. When the clay is almost dry, turn it over.

3 Carefully mould the clay into a plate-like shape between your thumbs and forefingers. Let the clay dry. Using the glue mix, cover the plate completely with pieces of coloured handmade paper.

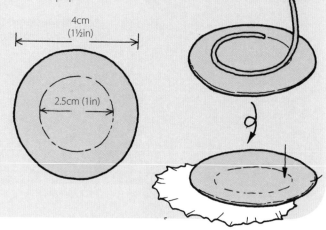

Fishbone

It's a well-known fact that cats love fish and this fishbone will certainly capture their interest.

1 Use a pencil, ruler and scissors to mark, measure and cut out a 3cm (1⅛in) square of white handmade paper and two 1.5 x 3cm (⅝ x 1⅛in) rectangles of blue-grey handmade paper. Using the glue mix, attach the rectangles to either side of the square, so that they overlap the square's sides slightly. Treating all the pieces of paper as if they were one, fold and unfold in half from bottom to top.

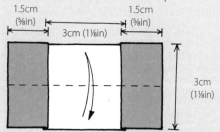

2 Smear glue mix all over the paper. Cut a 5cm (2in) length of 24-gauge white covered florists' wire and place it horizontally onto the centre of the paper's upper half. Fold the paper in half from bottom to top along the existing fold-line and press the edges neatly together.

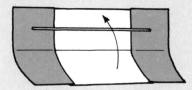

3 When the glue mix is dry, use a pencil and scissors to draw and cut out a fish-like shape, making sure to place the head and tail parts in the blue-grey sections of paper.

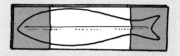

4 Use a black felt-tip pen to draw on the fish's eye. Cut out triangular pieces from the white section of paper, to suggest the fish's bones.

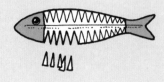

Cushion with Tassels

Pamper your cat with this cosy cushion, perfect for those afternoon naps.

1 Use a pencil, ruler and scissors to mark, measure and cut out four 0.5 x 1.5cm (³⁄₁₆ x ⁵⁄₈in) rectangles of coloured handmade paper.

2 Turn one rectangle lengthways on and cut a tiny fringe along its bottom edge. Be careful not to cut right through to the top edge. Roll the rectangle tightly up into a tassel. Repeat with the remaining three rectangles.

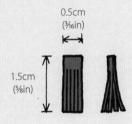

0.5cm (³⁄₁₆in)

1.5cm (⁵⁄₈in)

4 Place a tassel on top of the cushion's lower right-hand corner. Run a line of PVA adhesive along the diamond's adjacent edge and fold the adjoining corner in and over the cushion. Press down gently, so gluing the tassel in place.

3 Use a pencil, ruler and scissors to mark, measure and cut out a 10cm (4in) square of handmade paper in the same colour as the tassels. Make a cushion of cotton wool that is approximately 7cm (2³⁄₄in) square and 1cm (³⁄₈in) thick. Turn the square of handmade paper around to look like a diamond and place the cushion onto its centre, as shown. Fold the diamond's bottom corner up and over the cushion.

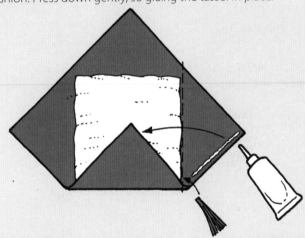

5 Repeat step 4 with the remaining three tassels, attaching one in each corner, while working anti-clockwise around the diamond.

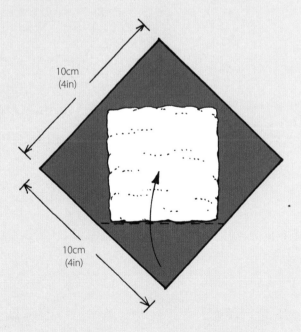

10cm (4in)

10cm (4in)

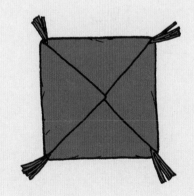

Suppliers

The best approach to gather the materials you will need to make pebble pets is to keep on the lookout and build up your collection gradually over time. Your local craft shop can order a particular product for you, give advice about your purchases, and may offer regular craft clubs and workshops. The Internet gives access to a wider choice of suppliers from all over the world. Here are the details of a few suppliers to get you started.

United Kingdom

C & H Fabrics Ltd
Head Office
Stone House
21/23 Church Road
Tunbridge Wells
Kent TN1 1HT
Tel: 01892 773612
Email: sales@candhfabrics.co.uk
www.candh.co.uk
For a huge selection of craft products. Click the link on their homepage to find your local store.

Falkiner Fine Papers
76 Southampton Row
London WC1B 4AR
Tel: 020 7831 1151
Email: falkiner@ic24.net
Supplier of handmade paper. Mail order available.

HobbyCraft Group Limited
Head Office
7 Enterprise Way
Aviation Park
Bournemouth International Airport
Christchurch
Dorset BH23 6HG
Tel: 01202 596100
www.hobbycraft.co.uk
Art and craft superstore. Click the link on their homepage to find your local store.

London Graphic Centre
16/18 Shelton Street
Covent Garden
London WC2H 9JL
Tel: 020 7759 4500
www.londongraphics.co.uk
Stationery, graphic and fine art retailer.

Paperchase
213–215 Tottenham Court Road
London W1T 7PS
Tel: 020 7467 6200
www.paperchase.co.uk
Handmade paper and art and craft supplier. Click the link on their homepage to find your local store.

USA

Fascinating Folds
PO Box 10070
Glendale
AZ 85318
www.fascinating-folds.com
An extensive supplier of reference materials for paper art and craft.

Michaels Stores Inc
8000 Bent Branch Drive
Irving
TX 75063
www.michaels.com
Carries a comprehensive selection of art and craft materials. Click the link on their homepage to find your local store.

Europe

Kars Creative Wholesale
Industrieweg 27
Industrieterrein 'De Heuning'
Postbus 97
4050 EB Ochten
The Netherlands
Tel: +31 (0) 344 642864
Email: info@kars.nl
www.kars.nl
Wholesaler of a vast range of craft materials.

Canada

The Paper Place
887 Queen St. West
Toronto
Ontario
Canada M6J 1G5
www.thepaperplace.ca
Retail supplier of Japanese handmade papers.

Australia

Japanese Paper and Origami Supplies
PO Box 558
Summer Hill
NSW 2130
Email: sales@origami.com.au
www.origami.com.au
Supplier of Japanese handmade paper.

About the Authors

Steve Biddle is an author, entertainer and origami expert. He studied in Japan with the top Japanese origami masters where he acquired a deeper knowledge of a subject that had always fascinated him. He is also a member of the most famous magical society in the world, The Magic Circle, holding the degree of Associate of The Inner Magic Circle with Silver Star.

Megumi Biddle is a graphic artist, designer and illustrator with a long-standing interest in papercrafts and doll-making. At the 1985 All Japan Handicraft Art Society's exhibition, held in the Tokyo Art Museum, she received the society's top debut award for developing her own unique style of doll-making. She is also a highly skilled silhouette artist and has cut out the profiles of many well-known celebrities.

Steve and Megumi have presented their 'Paper Magic' act at a variety of functions and taken their act across the world, performing in Europe, Australia, the USA and Japan. They have appeared on many television programmes, including *Blue Peter* and *The Generation Game* in the UK. Together, they have designed items for television, films and advertising campaigns, and produced many highly successful craft and picture books both for children and adults, including *Paper: Fold It* and *Paper Creations, Cards and Gifts* for D&C. They live on the south coast of England with Hana, their Japanese Akita dog.

Acknowledgments

We would like to thank the following people: Doreen and Caroline Montgomery for reviewing the text. A special thank you to our Akita and hamsters and to the following people whose pets gave us inspiration when creating the projects in *Pebble Pets*: Mayumi and Clive Bailey, Ben Brooks, Rachael Brown, Sue and Doug Brown, Donna and Ian Carter, Erico Kimura and Kayleigh Sparks. Finally, we would like to express our gratitude to the David & Charles editorial and design teams.

Index